The Antiegalitarian Mutation

The Antiegalitarian Mutation

The Failure of Institutional Politics in Liberal Democracies

NADIA URBINATI
AND ARTURO ZAMPAGLIONE

Translated by Martin Thom

COLUMBIA UNIVERSITY PRESS
New York

Columbia University Press
Publishers Since 1893
New York   Chichester, West Sussex
cup.columbia.edu

Originally published in Italy as *La mutazione antiegualitaria. Intervista sullo stato della democrazia*, a cura di A. Zampaglione
Italian edition copyright © 2013, Gius. Laterza & Figli. All rights reserved.
Revised and expanded English translation copyright © 2016 Columbia University Press
All rights reserved

Library of Congress Cataloging-in-Publication Data
Names: Urbinati, Nadia, 1995– author. | Zampaglione, Arturo, author.
Title: The antiegalitarian mutation : the failure of institutional politics in liberal democracies / Nadia Urbinati and Arturo Zampaglione; translated by Martin Thom.
Other title: Mutazione antiegualitaria. English
Description: New York : Columbia University Press, 2016. |
Includes index. | Translation of: la mutazione antiegualitaria.
Identifiers: LCCN 2015044779 | ISBN 9780231169844 (cloth : alk. paper) |
ISBN 9780231541930 (e-book)
Subjects: LCSH: Democracy—Western countries. | Social change—Political aspects—Western countries. | Western countries—Politics and government—21st century.
Classification: LCC JC423.U77513 2016 | DDC 320.01/1—dc23
LC record available at http://lccn.loc.gov/201504479

Columbia University Press books are printed on permanent and durable acid-free paper.
This book is printed on paper with recycled content.
Printed in the United States of America

c 10 9 8 7 6 5 4 3 2 1

COVER DESIGN: Milenda Nan Ok Lee

Contents

The Antiegalitarian Mutation

Introduction

Arturo Zampaglione

Over a span of a hundred years, two vastly different U.S. presidents chose Osawatomie, a small settlement located at the confluence of two rivers in southern Kansas, as an emblem of their country's bond of solidarity. In Osawatomie, whose name is a compound of two Native American tribes, the Osage and the Pottawatomie, both presidents spoke of the common good as a higher value than the preferences of the isolated individual.

In a speech that is often quoted as an example of presidential eloquence, on August 31, 1910, Theodore Roosevelt, a Republican president, for the first time explicitly warned the United States against its libertarian temptations: only a strong government, he argued, would be able to regulate the economy and guarantee social justice. It was again in Osawatomie that, on December 6, 2011, Barack Obama, a Democratic president, voiced his most passionate denunciation of rising economic inequality. "This is the defining issue of our time," Obama thundered, to rapturous applause. "This is a make-or-break moment for the middle class, and for all those who are fighting to get into the middle class."[1]

While political analysts from across the spectrum interpreted his words as touching a populist chord,[2] in raising the issue of inequality Obama was in fact echoing a language of protest: a protest that started in the Middle East as a cry against autocracy and injustice and then spread to many other areas of the world where the issue of rising economic inequality became a focus point. From Tahrir Square in Cairo, Egypt, to the Indignados (Outraged) of the Iberian Peninsula, from Zuccotti Park, next to Wall Street in lower Manhattan, to the Pearl Roundabout, a crossroads on the outskirts of the business district in Manama, Bahrain, the same matrix of discontent rallied crowds of disenfranchised, oppressed, and unemployed citizens who, under the banner of "occupation," did the opposite of populism: they reclaimed ownership of the public, by the public, and for the benefit of the public.

This book was born from the need to understand the significance of this complex and incendiary context, which was set against the background of the fragmentation and seeming privatization of the democratic agenda, embraced by secessionist and xenophobic movements all over the planet. The task of framing a response to the emergence of such contradictory forces in our time was what drove a journalist like me, seasoned by more than twenty years as the New York correspondent for *La Repubblica*, the largest Italian newspaper, to seek the learned opinion of Nadia Urbinati. A professor at Columbia University and a leading political theorist, Urbinati is a keen observer of political dynamics on both sides of the Atlantic who, as public intellectual on the pages of my newspaper, has sought to continue the tradition of political and social critique championed by Antonio Gramsci.

Conducted in New York, Bologna, and Rome, the peripatetic conversations collected in *The Antiegalitarian Mutation* explore Urbinati's assessment of contemporary democracy, which she sees as deeply threatened by a twofold challenge: rising socioeconomic inequality and divisive identity politics. These are certainly separate phenomena, but, as the six chapters that make up this book progressively clarify, they are not wholly disconnected. Just how long, Urbinati asks again and again, can democracy fail to resist the increase in inequality and poverty without becoming distorted? And for how long will democracy be able to withstand the pressure of all the political movements that call for the exclusion, rather than the inclusion, of entire segments of the world population without transmuting into something other than itself? And finally, why is it in the name of prepolitical entities, such as ethnicity, the ancestral bond with a territory, or blind allegiance to a specific interpretation of a sacred text, that exclusion is desired? The "antiegalitarian mutation" that Urbinati describes here, in a language as accessible as it is rigorous and nuanced, does not point to the wholesale disappearance of constitutional rights. This is the alarming prediction that another prominent Italian political theorist, Giorgio Agamben, has made regarding the transformation of democracy into a kind of totalitarian tyranny, not least because of the manner in which American democracy, in the aftermath of the attacks of September 11, 2001, seemed to abjure its loyalty to constitutional principles in the name of the "exceptional" threat of terrorism.[3] Unlike Agamben, Urbinati sees democracy as in danger of mutating rather than shrinking and in the end destroying itself. This "mutation," which she expands on more pointedly in chapter 1, has to do with a kind of hijacking of the democratic agenda by elitist enclaves and nationalist ideologies, which are well on the way to turning its universalist aspirations into particularistic projects. The issue of socioeconomic inequality, coupled with the practice of identitarian segregation, plays a key role in the increasing privatization and intrinsic perversion of democratic life.

But what is democracy for Urbinati? The conceptual underpinning of *The Antiegalitarian Mutation* is a nonteleological and antiperfectionist understanding of democracy, the clarification of which is key to the many topics populating our conversations. These include some of the classic questions of political theory, such as the meaning of democratic citizenship and the different brands of cosmopolitanism, but also more empirical issues, like the urgent migratory crises exploding along the borders of the global North; the future of the welfare model, especially in Europe; and the true meaning of meritocracy in late capitalism.

For Urbinati, democracy does not harbor a predetermined goal, as is the case for Francis Fukuyama and other theorists broadly located in the Hegelian tradition, for whom democracy is a teleological finality, a stage of development that political communities will eventually evolve into, mostly for their own good. And for Urbinati democracy is also not an ideal, a standard of perfection that shapes our conception of the good life, as political philosophers like Martha Nussbaum and Charles Larmore would have it. Alongside John Rawls and Jürgen Habermas, Urbinati takes democracy to be a matter of the legitimacy of the procedures that underlie its legal and political institutions as well as the deliberative processes that structure its decision making. This is the focus of chapter 2, in which Urbinati articulates the intellectual background from which her proceduralist vision originates, deriving from an empiricist tradition of reflection on democracy initiated by Alexis de Tocqueville and refined by John Stuart Mill and Quentin Skinner.

On the normative level, however, Urbinati's proceduralist leanings have been influenced by the legal formalism of Hans Kelsen, principally through the version of liberal socialism endorsed by Carlo Rosselli and Norberto Bobbio, both of whom loom large on Urbinati's horizon. Their conception of democracy as revolving around the value of political freedom is key to many of the positions that Urbinati expresses in this book and is most robustly expounded in chapter 3. In dialogue with the father of moral universalism, Immanuel Kant, but also with figures who are going to be less familiar to an American audience, including the inspirer of Italian unification, Giuseppe Mazzini, Urbinati presents a view of democracy that is grounded in the hard work of establishing relations of equal political freedom among citizens who are different in many respects but whose citizenship, taken in the broadest and most inclusive sense of that term, involves full participation in the life of the polity.

In line with her nonteleological and antiperfectionist approach, Urbinati does not make any promises concerning when and whether justice and equality could eventually be served. Rather, she articulates a set of "situated" conditions aimed at the progressive and indefinite rectification of social and economic inequality. Because of its rootedness in the present, this conception of democracy owes an intellectual debt to the immanent social critique inaugurated by Theodor W. Adorno and Max Horkheimer. But by providing political guarantees for social cooperation between actual and potential conflicting interests, this view of democracy is also endowed with the expectation of imparting legitimacy to power. Jean-Jacques Rousseau's 1755 *Discourse on Inequality* is Urbinati's point of departure on this issue because of her firm belief that equality is not a natural given: "Laying a hand on the normative order—that is, upon the institutions and upon their justifications—is what men and women should seek to do to live together as free persons. This, two and a half centuries later, is still our challenge" (chapter 1).

While she does not endorse a historical teleology, Urbinati is a staunch believer in the emancipatory power of democracy, which she defines as "a process of diffusion of political power" (chapter 1). This diffusion holds an ethical dimension, as "democracy is not merely a form of government . . . it is also a way of thinking our relationships with others and above all with ourselves. Saying that we must treat others with dignity and that each person is deserving of respect is, if one thinks carefully about it, a recognition of our own value through the recognition of the value of others" (chapter 2). Thus, democracy is both a system of procedures and norms and a political practice by which ordinary citizens form, express, and try to actualize their views on how to live together under the same laws.

Throughout this book, democracy emerges as a transformative force not only in a public and collective sense but also at the individual and subjective level. "Being democratic citizens means being capable of reasoning in terms of wide-ranging and general perspectives, in which we do not reflect only ourselves or those whom we deem equal to us because they have the same tastes but possibly many others and ideally everyone. Living as democratic citizens prepares us for putting ourselves in others' shoes, for making an effort not to reduce the world to ourselves, for understanding forms of life or life choices different from our own" (chapter 1). This complex transformation of the individual may be perhaps imagined as the result of what Bobbio understood as the modus operandi of democratic institutions: instructing citizens in freedom ("*educare i cittadini alla libertà*").

As for Bobbio, who is perhaps the Italian thinker who influenced Urbinati the most during her formative years, so, too, in *The Antiegalitarian Mutation* democracy is a way of reasoning, not just a set of arguments about how to govern. Without its *forma mentis*, which consists in learning how to appreciate the reasons of the other, we won't succeed in welcoming those whom we do not recognize as equals, including migrants and asylum seekers, legal and illegal residents. As we sat down to talk, in New York, Bologna, and Rome, the hundreds of thousands of human beings who every day gather at the borders of the global North and try to cross its political frontiers, whether by foot, across the desert in Arizona and New Mexico, or by boat, across the Mediterranean Sea, to land on the Italian island of Lampedusa or in the Spanish town of Tarifa, haunted our conversations from beginning to end. As we moved from topic to topic, we kept telling each other that maintaining democracy as an experience of openness to the other is one of the challenges presented by the mutation that is the focus of this book.

The examples that punctuate our exchange are a testimony to the spontaneous nature of the interview. Some derive from the Italian context and will broaden the English-speaking reader's horizon of reference. For instance, in chapter 6, we discuss a case that came before the Bologna court in the summer of 2011. It concerns whether a Roma girl, living with her family in a camp on the outskirts of the city, attending school only irregularly, and facing exploitation if not outright abuse, should be removed from the family and provided with a stable home environment as well as an education, which in Italy is compulsory. As a token of respect for the nomadic tradition of Roma tribes, the girl was left to live with her parents, a decision that Urbinati objected to, seeing it as an example of making justice serve a communitarian interest before or instead of that of the individual person (in this case, the acquiring of a basic education).

Some of the other examples given in this book, referring as they do to the domains of anthropology and sociology, will prompt its readers to reflect. This is the case with gated communities (chapter 1), which have spread around the globe in a variety of forms and to which Urbinati attributes a role as agents in the fragmentation of a shared sense of the polity. "Gated communities are not directly linked to the need for security, even if that was their justification when they first appeared, around thirty years ago. . . . Gated communities are a pioneering example of the secession of the few from the 'wider' society, anticipating one of the most striking aspects of the oligarchical mutation that we are today experiencing in every Western country." Drawing upon her classical formation and ongoing engagement with canonical political thinkers from Plato to Marx, Urbinati interprets the gated communities as a modern distillation of the "Spartan model" of citizenship, "in the sense that their members are like the citizens of the ancient Greek city, free because and inasmuch as they are socially or ethnically equal." She uses the model of the gated community to analyze the claims of secessionist movements such as the Italian Northern League (Lega Nord). Like other secessionist movements around the world, the Northern League is based on a phenomenon of "appropriation of rights" that, in the name of equality and freedom, transforms the universalist aspirations of the "citizen" of a political community into the particularistic purview of the "member" of a private association.

The issue of how to defend those whose rights are threatened is, however, not limited to the exclusionary claims of the gated communities, to the secessionist movements, or even to nation-states. Political and economic instability creates warlike conditions that, coupled with global interdependence and instant communication, transform segments of specific populations into refugees and migrants. Since Immanuel Kant's seminal 1795 essay *Perpetual Peace*, the debate on cosmopolitanism has sought to find a way of extending human rights, especially the right of movement, to the entire population of the globe. The concept of universalism and its cosmopolitan translation form the Kantian framework that Urbinati embraces to answer this question and that occupy the bulk of chapter 3.

No doubt, the 1948 United Nations Universal Declaration of Human Rights, the 1957 Treaty of Rome, and the rest of the complex fabric of humanitarian legislation have been inspired by Kantian principles. Yet, as Urbinati recalls, "the juridical order in which domestic and international politics are given their structure is founded upon the state and cannot countenance a political identity outside of the state: not even a European one, which does however aspire to become supranational. Yet these migrants lay claim to the dignity of political speech and advance a demand to be autonomous protagonists, in the name of themselves as human beings: they cry out for what until today has been a utopia, in other words, a cosmopolitan form of political right." Urbinati considers this demand for the right to be a political agent, which in Kant's language amounts to cosmopolitan citizenship, to be an "important novelty" of the contemporary situation, which comes into full view at the borders of the global North and represents "an important challenge to the progressive and democratic forces of Europe" (chapter 3).

Urbinati is stringent in her evaluation of the European Union as an experiment of a new political agent: as it stands, she argues, it is nothing more than a myth or, even worse, a product of cosmopolitan propaganda. But throughout our conversations, as she delved deeply into the debate on cosmopolitanism, which she considers essential in containing the most destructive effects of the antiegalitarian mutation, she became more hopeful that the future might hold a European promise.

In her reconstruction, there are two kinds of cosmopolitanism: one, most influenced by the liberal and libertarian approach, interprets the site of democracy to be civil society. In this view, endorsed, for example, by Richard Falk, democracy is a civic culture of mobilization and participation in which grassroots movements are held to contain more democratic power than the procedures of decision making. A second view of cosmopolitanism, which Urbinati herself defends, does not ✓ advocate a "poststate" approach but rather a "postnational" one. Articulated by Daniele Archibugi and Étienne Balibar, this "democratic cosmopolitanism" holds that if left to its own devices, civil society can become the source of new forms of discrimination, injustice, and oppression. To a large extent this is exactly what is happening today with the antiegalitarian mutation. As Urbinati sees it, "democratic cosmopolitanism ought to take it upon itself to engage on this front, in order to devise new institutions and new norms that protect whoever is not part of a state but only a member of humanity, if one can put it like that" (chapter 3). Whether the European Union, if it were to complete its process of constitutionalization, could become a truly new institution able to protect whoever is not a member of a state remains an open question.

The central presupposition of democratic cosmopolitanism, embraced by Urbinati, that civil society needs regulation because if left to itself it may produce greater inequality, is the starting point of the most comprehensive and most influential economic analysis of inequality today, and maybe of all time: Thomas Piketty's *Capital in the Twenty-First Century*. Capitalism, according to Piketty, "automatically generates arbitrary and unsustainable inequalities that radically undermine the meritocratic values on which democratic societies are based." More specifically, Piketty identifies the danger of what he calls the "forces of divergence," which can emerge "even in a world where there is adequate investment in skills and where all the conditions of 'market efficacy' . . . appear to be satisfied." Not only may top earners easily become a class all to themselves, sharply separated from the rest of the workforce, but there is a set of forces of divergence that are specifically associated with the way in which capital accumulates when economic growth is weak and returns on capital are high. In other words, "when the rate of return on capital significantly exceeds the growth rate of the economy . . . then it logically follows that inherited wealth grows faster than output and income."[4]

If for Piketty one of the main forces of divergence coincides with inherited wealth and its consequent privileges because they stifle the agonistic model that since Adam Smith has been shown to regulate capitalism, then for Urbinati one of the main forces of divergence is labor, which she deems intimately connected with the concepts of political equality and individual freedom. This discussion of labor, which occupies the bulk of chapter 4, is at the center of what Urbinati calls the historical compromise between the few and the many. In her mind, there is no dignity without the possibility of seeing in one's labor a way not only to satisfy one's material needs but also to make one's mark and express one's talents and capacities. "The dignity of the person and a dignified labor have given rise to the ethical world of modern democracies, a world in which needs and rights are intertwined." Democratic citizenship is thus based on the eradication of poverty, aptly renamed "unemployment."

A recurring question of *The Antiegalitarian Mutation* is what happens to democratic citizenship when labor is increasingly deprived of rights and when the risk of poverty, through unemployment, becomes a structural condition of life. This is a new condition of our age and a grave threat to democratic agency. "Short-term contracts often pave the way to future poverty. Work without rights is a passport to destitution. The present has just as many risks, not only because there is an objective diminution in employment opportunities but also because of the practice of accepting work without rights, work for the present, without any assurances for the future. Propaganda against tenured jobs—for the most part orchestrated by those who, like university professors and economists, already have them—leaves one speechless. As we know, ideologies help us swallow bitter pills" (chapter 4).

The antiegalitarian mutation is thus also the end of a compromise between democracy and capitalism that is at the foundation of the modern state but that in Western societies has been profoundly changed by the experience of World War II. In the aftermath of the greatest carnage in human history and its most explicit genocidal endeavor, the self-understanding of Western democracies was reborn around the need to vaccinate the political system against both tyranny and "collective impoverishment" (chapter 4). But since the 1980s, this noble project, in which the "culture of solidarity" was a key factor, has been drastically undermined. Chapter 5 explores the perverse alliance between market forces and particular interests, which is exemplified by a detailed discussion of the debate, both in the United States and in Italy, on the public funding of private and religious schools.

On this point Urbinati parts company with Piketty and other theorists who claim that inequality is a structural condition of capitalism. For Urbinati, the antiegalitarian mutation also has political roots. The central theme of an ideological war against the welfare state and its social-democratic ideology, and the consequent erosion of equality, is the child of the neoliberal turn, for which she provides a precise and far-reaching genealogy. Not only economists such as Milton Friedman but also liberal thinkers such as Friedrich Von Hayek and political philosophers such as Robert Nozick contributed within their own domains to the paradigm shift of the antiegalitarian mutation, an ideological program that was able to reverse the direction of state policies and obtain widespread consent in Western democracies. Politically, however, neoliberalism does, of course, bear the mark of two Anglo-American leaders: Ronald Reagan in the United States and Margaret Thatcher, the conservative prime minister of the United Kingdom. Urbinati is crystal clear on this point: Reagan and Thatcher launched a radical project of disavowal of political guarantees, the effect of which was collective impoverishment. The two political leaders overturned a process and a way of thinking that since World War II had sustained the policies of redistribution and social justice at the heart of the welfare state.

These forces of fragmentation and privatization of the public interest challenge the principles of equal respect and opportunity that enable democracy as "a work of permanent correction, founded upon the pragmatic idea that imperfections and limits pertain to all human beings without exception and that the learning process advances by trial and error and with the aid of others" (chapter 2). This appeal to a pragmatic approach to political theory runs deep in the fabric of Urbinati's arguments and stems from her studies of John Stuart Mill.[5] For her, democracy "is a political system best characterized as a site of fallibility and mutability. Which is precisely why freedom of speech and the free expression of dissent, along with participation in the process of deliberation" are absolutely essential (chapter 2). In chapter 6, the book concludes with the need to distinguish between a "politics of difference," whose objective is the always amendable universalist ideal of equality, and the social particularism of "identity politics," which promotes special treatment for given ethnic, religious, and other groups. These kinds of claims about the inequality of the social body are at the very root of the fragmentation and privatization that undermine the future of democracy as we have known it, imagined it, and dreamed of it until today.

We are all children of our time, and we become aware of our context through its critical examination, which transforms the environment that was assigned to us by chance into an environment that belongs to us by choice. This is a difficult process that anchors our self-knowledge in self-respect while making possible our respect for others, whom we understand as having gone down a similar path in order to become who they are. It is this very possibility that is threatened by the antiegalitarian mutation and that Urbinati and I urge our readers to reclaim.

NOTES

1. http://www.whitehouse.gov/the-press-office/2011/12/06/remarks-president-economy-osawatomie-kansas.

2. Surprisingly enough, even the liberal press read President Obama's foregrounding of economic inequality as a populist move, including the *New York Times*, which titled the story covering the Osawatomie Remarks "Obama Strikes Populist Chord with Speech on GOP Turf." http://www.nytimes.com/2011/12/07/us/politics/obama-strikes-populist-chord-with-speech-in-heartland.html.

3. Giorgio Agamben, *State of Exception* (Chicago: University of Chicago Press, 2008).

4. Thomas Piketty, *Capital in the Twenty-First Century* (Cambridge, Mass.: Harvard University Press, 2014), 1, 23, 26.

5. See Nadia Urbinati, *Mill on Democracy: From the Athenian Polis to Representative Government* (Chicago: University of Chicago Press, 2002).

1

A Great Mutation

Q. *The world has finally overcome the worst financial crisis since the Great Depression. The collective trauma seems to have changed many things, not only in the economy, by opening the way to new rules and expectations, dubbed "the new normal," but also in politics and society. Rising inequalities and mass migrations are arguably feeding a "democracy fatigue" in Italy and other Western countries, as shown by opinion polls and electoral results.*

I want to begin our conversation by asking you for an assessment of the "state" of our democracies. How strong is it? And what is really changing?

A. Our democracy is undergoing a process of molecular mutation, although this is occurring in various contexts and emitting a range of different signals. We venture interpretations, but its overall direction still eludes us. In its more visible aspect, the mutation is political and economic. It concerns not only the mode of conceiving rights and duties, the use and the functioning of the institutions, and the sense of being part of a political collective but also the social composition of citizenship, the relationship between classes, and the political management of the economy. Above all else, it manifests itself as a mutation in an antiegalitarian direction. In its more visible aspect, the mutation is cultural and moral and presents itself as the identitary (or communitarian) appropriation of civil liberties that written constitutions declare should be distributed equally. Possessive ideology seems to have spread its wings to cover the political system, in the form of hostility toward anyone who is different and of closure against anyone who is not "like us." This is particularly visible in Europe, where the first great crisis of the new century has put into question the linking of democracy with pluralism, the tie upon which constitutional democracy was established after World War II. The epithet of possession—above all in its communitarian (or nationalist) sense, as "ours"—seems to have acquired an unwonted preponderance and now to enjoy a presumption of legitimacy that cannot help but trouble anyone who believes in democracy.

If, moreover, we turn to the sphere of private life and then again to intellectual, social, and political changes, we soon discover a greater distance between persons as regards the opportunities they have to acquire actual and symbolic goods, among them recognition and the power to make decisions or to influence those elected to make them. Access to these goods is ever more selective for a growing number of persons and ever more concentrated in certain classes and in certain parts of the world. The slogan devised by the people who, from September 2011 onward gave rise in Zuccotti Park (New York City) to Occupy Wall Street, casts light upon this unease: it is 1 percent (perhaps less) of the population, or the richest part of the world, that dictates the goals and constraints to democratic governments and that de facto rules.

Q. *What is happening to democracy if even in the advanced industrialized countries the majority of citizens feel powerless? And how should we define a political system in which the voice of the minority is louder than that of the majority?*

A. In an essay from 1984, *The Future of Democracy: A Defence of the Rules of the Game*, Norberto Bobbio, one of the Italian political thinkers best known to Anglo-American scholars, wrote that the Western democracies have won the contest with the socialist democracies over the rights of liberty but not over the questions that concern the equality of social conditions and hence of the opportunities for enjoying those rights. Demonstrating that the rights of liberty are at the basis of the democracy of the moderns—Bobbio concludes—has been a fundamental but incomplete victory: it has still to be proved that politics is capable of limiting the impact of social inequalities. It has still to be proved that democracy is capable of promoting effectively social justice and an equalizing of basic social resources. In the two decades after World War II, the constitutional democracies of Western Europe sought to resolve this dilemma, defying on the one hand the socialist democracies of Eastern Europe and on the other hand minimalist American democracy, what was known as liberal democracy. After the fall of the Berlin Wall, the European Union has proclaimed itself the legitimate heir of this project of social and political democracy. But things are changing rapidly and not for the better.

This unresolved challenge allows us to glimpse troubling scenarios. The established democracies are today weaker and less sure of their own strength than they were three decades ago, when Bobbio was writing. Once the challenge with state socialism in the name of individual liberty had been won, Western democracies, which were the offspring of that idea of liberty, found themselves facing a problem far more fraught with consequences. As Claus Offe has recently argued, the social-democratic project has become as obsolete as the paradigm it relied upon. That project presumed the centrality of political identity (citizenship) and thus an asymmetry of power between the forum and the market, so that the former was *"allowed*, in fact *intended*, to have an impact" on the latter and interfere with it if need be. Yet once the social-democratic paradigm had gone into decline, the liberal-pluralist one also proved to be weak. The liberal-pluralist paradigm is predicated upon a self-enforcing equilibrium between political identity and social identity, thus a symmetrical relation between forum and market that forbids the former to intervene in the organization of the latter. The defeat of the liberal-pluralist paradigm reveals how utopian it is to suppose that economic power can be entirely unfettered or unregulated and not upset the democratic order. This proves that social constructs (and the forum and the market are both socially constructed, not natural) do not produce any equilibrium spontaneously. A decision has thus to be made on which of the two domains we choose, our choice revealing our normative principle. If liberty as autonomy for the greater number is our principle, we cannot but give priority to politics and conceive the relationship between the forum and the market as an asymmetrical one. The historical experience of the last two and a half centuries confirms this view and shows that a constitutional democracy can be more conducive to autonomy for the many than an unregulated market. Today, with the decline of the social-democratic model and the impotence of the liberal-pluralistic one, we see that the challenge to liberty issues on the one hand from economic liberty and on the other hand from the rise of identitary (or communitarian) conceptions of popular sovereignty, which is most of the time a refuge that impoverished citizens seek in the attempt to protect their scarce resources against an open access to social benefits. Thus the conflicting relationship between democracy and capitalism upsets also the relationship between democracy and universalism. This is in my view the reason why the risk of identitary democracy is high today, in the sense that the relationship between democracy and universalism is once again central yet more problematic, less certain and self-evident, and finally more difficult to sustain and defend. For once, *facticity* seems to prevail over *normativity*, thus relegating democracy to the rank of an ideology that the leading class orchestrates to make the vast majority believe that they are themselves responsible for their choices. Who is to be blamed if not the sovereign citizens?

Q. *Can one say that these changes run counter to democracy?*

A. Democracy is a process of diffusion of political power. Yet individuals, groups, and territories appear to be distancing themselves from one another and from those principles of equality and liberty that, from the eighteenth century onward, either through revolutions or through gradual transformations, spread across the whole of the West, shaping our everyday life.

Equality is an artificial or socially and culturally constructed value, not a natural one. It has crystallized in the course of history and through various contributions, classical and modern, secular and religious. Our awareness of it has brought our societies to a democratic form of government, the political system that more than any other is in agreement with equality. But now we seem to find ourselves in a democracy in which actual and material differences—of income, sex, age, religion, and ethnicity—are too readily becoming reasons for excluding, discriminating against, and treating in an unequal fashion. Let me be quite clear: the problem is not the differences as such, nor is it even all the inequalities, but the manner in which they translate into interpersonal relationships that generate an unequal distribution of basic power and moreover the power of political recognition.

In the *Discourse on the Origin and the Basis of Inequality Among Men*, first published in 1755, Jean-Jacques Rousseau wrote that, whereas all humans are naturally different in many respects (health, strength, sex, age, etc.), the transformation of differences into inequalities of power and of respect is a product of social relations, an artificial fact. Laying a hand on the normative order—that is, upon the institutions and upon their justifications—is what men and women should seek to do if they aspire to live together as free persons. This, two and a half centuries later, is still our challenge. As democratic citizens we make ourselves equal by law precisely because we know that we are different, and even unequal, in many respects; this artificial domain we construct, and to which we give the name of democratic citizenship, is like a shield that protects our individual specificity without at the same time precluding our making ourselves equal in political power and before the law.

It seems to me that the current antiegalitarian mutation challenges this traditional view and denotes a profound anguish in democracy: as if it were ever more difficult for citizens to live together under the same conditions, or to treat themselves as if they were equal in something immaterial and artificial yet so concrete and palpable that its absence or erosion is immediately felt, as if what was written in our constitutions or bills of rights some decades ago is ever more distant from our own material life, until at the last it loses purchase or salience. How distant can the norm be from actuality before its value diminishes in the eyes of those who should honor it? How firmly can a democracy resist the rise in social and economic inequality without suffering distortion?

Q. Our conversation will turn around this great "mutation," whose contours you have just delineated. The term "mutation" is borrowed from genetics, where it indicates the basic unfolding of evolutionary processes. Why have you sought to apply it to the political sphere?

A. I was looking for a term that did not suggest a predetermined process of a "from"/ "toward" kind, as if following a *telos*, a direction toward an already written outcome. In *The Great Transformation*, a seminal work written at a time of tragic crisis in Europe (1944), Karl Polanyi, a Hungarian historian of economics and a philosopher, attempted to explain the causes of that crisis in terms of the transformation of market society, interpreting it as a total change linked to the industrial revolution and the modern state.

Up until the outbreak of World War I, Polanyi explained, state and market had advanced side by side for decades, so much so that Western peoples nursed the illusion that they had found a functional equilibrium between peace and liberty. Yet the twentieth century witnessed the collapse of the equilibrium between the four pillars sustaining the nineteenth-century utopia of endless peace and progress. Two of the four pillars were economic and two political, two were international and two national: (a) the system of division and balancing of powers, which had kept the peace in Europe for some decades; (b) the gold standard as the foundation of global commercial exchanges; (c) a market that regulated itself and was capable of generating peace and increasing wealth; and (d) the constitutional and parliamentary liberal state.

The end of the equilibrium between these components had essentially been caused by the market (pillar c), whose mythical power of self-regulation had in reality engendered immiseration and inequality at home and colonialism and imperialism abroad: conditions that would in a few years lead to war within Europe and beyond instead of preserving peace and liberty as promised. Society as a great self-ruling market clashed with society ruled by states, and the struggle between state and market ended up fundamentally undermining the conditions of the nineteenth-century equilibrium. Obviously society had to defend itself from this disequilibrium, but every measure it took to defend itself clashed fatally with the theorem of self-regulation of the market. The tension, and finally the conflict between state and market, would materialize as the end of the liberal state and the birth of the authoritarian states, which subdued the whole of society.

World War II swept away in a short space of time an entire social and political order, but the causes lay concealed, according to Polanyi, in the system itself. The breakdown of the global economic order found expression as a global war because in that order there were the hidden causes of war; it involved an order that had reduced European society to a theater from which the complexity (or pluralism) of the ethical, cultural, religious, and moral factors that used to define its culture had been sacrificed to the worship of one factor only (the economic) and finally expunged. The causes of the decline lay in the latent effects of industrialization and of the birth of capitalist society, which had reduced the multiplicity of the factors of prosperity and stability to just one, that of profit. The unchecked advance of industrialization and consumerism, which signified an increase of wealth and of population, had breached the dykes and ended up jeopardizing that ideology of peace founded upon "liberal liberty" which had been affirmed in the 1830s, with the triumph of the constitutional system.

According to Polanyi's key idea, the free market, for some decades identified with the spread of peace and of diplomatic relations among formerly inimical states, had altered the texture of society, encountering wholly predictable resistance. The power of international finance, which had initially grown in the shadow of state nonintervention, expanded so far and so much that it required a strong state, one militarily prepared and ready to protect the extraterritorial action of the market. That was the trajectory from old market liberalism to the collapse of liberty and peace that marked European states from the second half of the nineteenth century up until World War I. According to Polanyi, for generations Europeans had been used to identifying commerce with peace, and then, faced with the scenarios of world war, they failed to see that the order of the market and of finance contained the very conditions for that transformation. This outcome, he thought, was a preordained consequence of the history of industrial capitalistic civilization.

Q. What does the order elucidated by Polanyi involve? And at what point are we in the process of adaptation?

A. Although I hesitate to speak of a holistic or wholesale transformation of the capitalistic order, some mutations can be detected and identified, especially if we shine a spotlight at the public and political sphere, adopting a point of view that is "internal" to the democratic order. What I propose to do is to follow the traces of democratic principles, observing how they are interwoven with the social conditions, ✔ or how they alter. I start out, however, from one premise: "a-teleology" is a constitutive aspect of democracy, which does not promise us an ideal world, or the realization of a utopia, and not even, as we shall see in what follows, unequivocally correct or good decisions. I would thus wish to respect its nonperfectionistic nature and for this reason adopt a perspective of alteration or mutation.

Q. What do you mean by "perspective of alteration"?

A. It means collecting together signals of mutation without ranking them as indicators of an intelligent or preordained plan. I repeat:

democracy does not guarantee us a superior order of life or a perfect society. It does not even guarantee us a society of equals. Its function consists in striving to reconcile political liberty and social diversity and civil peace, to so arrange things that, becoming citizens, persons who are different in their opinions and social situations, in their beliefs and aspirations, in their lifestyles and preferences, live together in mutual respect, within a legal and political system of equally distributed rights and duties. A democratic society is cacophonic rather than homogeneous. I insist upon this reading, which is anchored to rules and procedures, because it is precisely starting out from such an approach, at first sight very minimalist, that the mutation most clearly comes into view. By contrast with other political regimes, Carlo Rosselli, the Italian antifascist political leader, wrote in the 1930s that democracy is not tied to the defense of any particular goal, as, for example, the hereditary transmission of power in monarchy or the protection of a social caste in an oligarchical regime. It does not indicate to us any object to attain, except for the implementation and the defense of criteria of discussion and decision making, which enable us to criticize and change all the decisions taken, and hence our social relationships themselves, with a view to honoring better the promise we have made to respect the principles of equal respect and opportunity in the power to give laws to ourselves. Democracy is seen, in short, as an unceasing work of adjustment, which is never immune from changes and also possible interruptions or withdrawals.

Precisely because it does not suggest a premeditated direction or timetable, it seems to me that the term "mutation" better enables us to bring out certain important alterations in this ceaseless "maintenance work" and to capture more precisely, and without catastrophism, the ideological bewilderment (*spaesamento*) of our time.

Q. Bewilderment? That is to say, loss of cultural identity?

A. Prior to the decline of the ideologies of the twentieth century there seemed to be (for those who embraced them) visions of ideal cities and, moreover, certain blueprints as to how to actualize them. Democracy was conceived in service to that perfectionist goal. Being certain of the goal entailed trusting in one's own strength of will and ultimately in one's readiness to make great sacrifices if needed in order to achieve it. Just as with religions, the dogma of the ideal city or the scientific certainty of the socialist society oriented individual choices untainted by any considerations of personal gratification, which is what generally serves as the motive force for individual action through time. It seemed that the future would surely exist in a tomorrow within reach of the doctrine and that political-social-cultural intervention, if consistent with the fundamental principles of that ideology, would bring that future about.

The decline of those kinds of ideological narrative has revealed the absence of reference points external to the actors' reason and to their will and has thereby exalted individual or group preferences, personal interests or those of the immediate neighborhood (community of proximity), or at any rate some specific points of view for the implementation of some specific objectives that were dear to the hearts of those involved. The domain of the present acquired more value than the domain of the future: this process of temporal redress proceeded along with the consolidation of democracy.

Q. In order to understand better the scope of the great mutation, can you give some examples of these phenomena, drawn from the political domain or from current affairs?

A. The first concerns the birth of political movements defending values "that exclude" and that are propounded in the name of certain prepolitical entities, as, for example, an ethnic group or an ancestral tie with a territory, like a nation or a set of traditions and beliefs. This is somehow what is happening in Europe with the rise of nationalisms and right-wing parties, which contest the project of European Union in the name of goods that are owned by some but not all, for example, national identity, the Christian religion, or cultural tradition. Sometimes, these values are declared—often in fact screamed—against the welfare state, against the system of shared rules that dispense social services, and against the principle of impartiality that the constitutional democracies incorporate in order to distribute costs and benefits according to the principle of fairness among citizens. The so-called ethnocentrists, that is, those who put their own local or regional or territorial group first, would have the norms follow the inequalities of belonging. In other words, they claim that the laws ought not to be responsible for ensuring that cultural or ethnic differences are not a cause of inequality in the enjoyment of rights. In the perspective of the "ethnocentrists," sociocultural identity should become the norm and be translated directly into the laws. It is a process that challenges the modern idea of rights, rejecting the generality and universality of the law, with the aim of interrupting abstract equality and privileging substantive equality, or those who are equal in something over and against the others. I would like to consider here the case of the Northern League (Lega Nord), which was born in the late 1980s, championing local distinctiveness, acquiring over the years a strong association with a particular kind of identity politics, and finally becoming, these days, a xenophobic and neofascist movement. The Northern League, like other such movements that have arisen in Europe in the last thirty years, should be read as a phenomenon of disassociation—cultural as well as political—of one part of the nation-state from the country as a whole and of one group of citizens from the wider community of citizens. It is a claim of national identity in its least political meaning, that is to say, an identity dissociated from political citizenship and legal equality and associated basically and first of all with some non- or prepolitical qualities. In the name of what? In the name of a determination no longer to share the same responsibilities, and hence the same costs or sacrifices, with all the other parts of the country, of the desire instead to safeguard their own diversity as the good that is most concrete and closest to hand and, or so they suppose, most valid. In this idea of canceling the distances between the "I" and the "we," democracy risks becoming a dangerously identitarian and antiliberal regime.

Q. *You, however, are not saying that those Italians who defend the interests of the northeast are not democratic.*

A. No, that would be mistaken. They interpret democracy (and first of all equality) in a way that works to their advantage as a group, against the interests of the larger political community if need be. They distort the idea of equality so that, rather than being a term that denotes a promise of a political and legal *relationship* between people who are strangers to one another, it is translated into the name of an essence, of a quality possessed by them and them alone: sociological equality rather than legal and political equality, and thus equality as a politics of affirmation and protection of a certain group against others who are not recognized as similar to them or capable of becoming so. So far as the aims of the followers of movements such as the Northern League are concerned, democracy becomes a militant politics of proximity or a project of cultural homogeneity. Advocates of identitarian democracy want the fundamental values of political equality to be restricted to their own people and their own territory. They want a sociological substance to be reflected in the laws. They want proximity and directness between their supposed cultural identity and the legal order of the state.

I suggest that we speak of the *appropriation* by identitary groups of principles that in fact had originally been wrested from, and defended against, identitary forms of political relations. In this sense the mutation assumes "repelling" and antiuniversalist characteristics. It displays a distortion of the meaning of sharing because it proposes the equality of equals in order to defend a good imagined as ancestral (one's own group, tradition, religion, social class). It seems to me that what we are seeing here is a refutation of the very idea of the generality of the law and of the autonomy of politics from the cultural and social conditions of existence. Indeed, the autonomy of political equality is what this mutation is about and is the reason why I propose to talk of an identitary appropriation of principles that, since after World War II in particular, have been interpreted as a strategy for the inclusion and emendation of all identitary projects. The lament, which we often hear, at the lack of any sense of the state or at the privatization of the public for the satisfaction of aims that are specific to a group or to certain persons is—if we look closely—an admission of the violation of the principle of the universality of the law and of justice as impartiality, or the autonomy of politics as an artificial endeavor to attain a generality of judgment and perspective.

Another example of the mutation, which is particularly evident in Italy (which is in this respect too an interesting laboratory of mutation), has to do with the assault on public schools.

Q *In the deliberations of the Italian Constituent Assembly, which from June 1946 to January 1948 wrote the Constitution of the Italian Republic (the first democratic constitution), schooling was defined as a fundamental right of the citizen and, more specifically, as a political right—not simply a social one. In what way does the mutation affect schools?*

A. School (basic schooling in particular) is not a social service: the specification is fundamental, in that every citizen needs to know in order to have the opportunity to decide reasonably, as the Italian constitutionalist Piero Calamandrei explained very well when he was a member of the Constituent Assembly.

Calamandrei's idea was neither original nor unique. Beginning with the birth of modern democracy, after the revolutions of the eighteenth century, creating a system of public schools was a goal shared by many thinkers and political leaders, from the Marquis de Condorcet to John Dewey, just to mention two of the best-known and most representative figures. Educating citizens has been a central project in democratic societies. Going to school is not only a right but a duty (at any rate during the years of compulsory attendance, which may vary from country to country) precisely because citizenship is a sovereign power whose exercise should be performed by all with responsibility and, hopefully, knowledge. Although democracy cannot countenance the idea of making the right to vote conditional upon citizens having their knowledge tested, yet it must want them not to be illiterate and to be endowed with some basic capacity for furthering their education. Public schooling has not been set up with the aim of regimenting the public (this was the distorted way in which fascism interpreted the meaning of public instruction) but in order to make possible the formation of citizens, persons capable of making autonomous choices and critical judgments not only in their private and social life but above all in politics. We should not forget that voting is a power that has direct effects upon everyone, and hence it is desirable that it be used with discretion or responsibility: even if no norm can impose a responsible vote (voting is perhaps the only irresponsible power in a democracy, being unaccountable and wholly arbitrary), it is possible to create the indirect conditions for this to happen. And public schools fulfill one of the most important indirect functions in the growth of public reason. It may be worth citing John Dewey, who wrote in *Democracy and Education* in 1938 (deliberately pitting democracy's notion of the public against the one advanced by totalitarian states in Europe) that democracy and education are in a reciprocal relation: "For it is not merely that democracy is itself an educational principle, but that democracy cannot endure, much less develop, without education in that narrower sense in which we ordinarily think of it, and especially as we think of it in the school."

Q. What is the significance of the "public reason" to which you refer here?

A. We mean a form of reflection made up of criteria of reasoning based on principles that define a democratic society and prompt us to act: to learn how to apply rights and duties when we judge on a given fact or behavior; to use a common grammar through which everyone can communicate, beyond the region in which they live and the family into which they were born and the religion they believe in; to develop wide-ranging public and moral judgments that transcend our specific conditions and make us capable of understanding others; and then also to distinguish between "what appears to me" and "what it is my duty to do," so that our political community may endure.

Being democratic citizens means being capable of reasoning in terms of wide-ranging and general perspectives, in which we do not reflect only ourselves or those whom we deem equal to us because they have the same tastes or beliefs but possibly many others and ideally everyone. Living as democratic citizens prepares us for putting ourselves in others' shoes, for making an effort not to reduce the world to ourselves, for understanding forms of life or life choices different from our own. When we say that an authoritative decision or a law is unjust, we mean that in our nonprofessional evaluation (since we are not under any obligation to be or to become lawyers and judges) that it is not general enough, that it does not reflect the interest of everyone because it is the reflection of certain ethical visions or of certain beliefs or of certain interests that have succeeded in winning, perhaps with the backing of a powerful propaganda machine, the consent of the majority. Now, public school is the first training ground, although not the only one nor the last, in which we train to be citizens, to transcend ourselves as specific subjects and to seek to cultivate a wide-ranging gaze, as Hannah Arendt wrote. Moreover, a public school is a place in which children from different religious, economic, and ethnic backgrounds meet and learn to interact and respect one another as actors within a larger community general enough to host all. Not to be segregated in our early education, to be exposed to the diverse world of others, is in and by itself a school of democratic citizenship. Public schooling is an opportunity to be educated in the broad sense of the term, not simply to be instructed and to learn.

Reflecting on the reasons for the failure of communitarian experiments in New England, Ralph Waldo Emerson observed in the mid–nineteenth century that each individual tends to devise ingenious strategies to protect himself from the gaze of others. Solitude, courtesy, good manners, etiquette, irony, and even sarcasm are expedients that each of us employs to render our skins thicker so as to check not so much the contamination of others as their inspection and curiosity, supervision, and censorship. Trust in ourselves thus plays a "hygienic" role, but—please note—not to protect a kind of pristine identity or a primordial authenticity but rather the actual freedom we have to alter our identity and opinion, to "contradict ourselves," if necessary, and to allow communication with others. This is the unpremeditated ethical goal that living together in a democratic community promotes.

Q. And that is why public schooling is a political right.

A. Yes, but in Italy (which is not an exception to this process of impoverishment of public schools) for the last two decades it has been under the crossfire of the two political groupings of the Left and the Right. So true is this that there has been the bipartisan reinterpretation of Article 33 of the Italian constitution on schooling, which claims that private schools are free to exist and operate but without being a burden on the public purse. We will come back, I hope, to the devious strategies recently adopted by Italian governments to bypass this constitutional article and give public money to private schools and to those families that choose a private school for their children. Here I propose that we return to the erosion of equality and other emblematic factors that concern, for instance, the role of cultural minorities in contemporary Europe. These are also examples that confirm the existence of a great mutation in our time.

Q. We shall undoubtedly return to this topic in the course of our conversation. But allow me to point out that in Italy, until recently, the barometer of democracy and equality has not always indicated good weather. Compulsory schooling ended at fourteen, whereas the minimum age at which you could vote was twenty-one. In the workplace, as with pensions and healthcare issues, rights were certainly not what they are today. What does this mean? Do contradictory phenomena, pushing in opposite directions, perhaps exist?

A. We can speak of the coexistence of processes of democratization and of phenomena that instead block democratization. On the one hand there is the expansion of juridical conditions of equal respect and of equal opportunity; on the other hand there are strong countervailing economic, social, and even cultural impulses, which arise as a contrary reaction. It is as if to the expansion of liberty there corresponded a contrary force of identitary resistance.

It is true that from the end of World War II onward there has been a broadening of political rights, exemplified by the lowering of the age at which citizens are entitled to exercise the right to vote and by the inclusion of women in citizenship (in Italy and France, this happened in 1946). But that has proceeded in conjunction with the exclusion of other people, for example, immigrants or those who, although not being national (or Italian, in this case) by birth, could aspire to citizenship and to the right to vote by virtue of their long residence in the country. The democratization of domestic societies seems to be accompanied by a phenomenon involving the protection of the included through strategies of exclusion. The more that citizens came to feel the value of their citizenship, the more they thought it legitimate to interpret it as a privilege to be protected. This may perhaps explain the decision to raise walls that keep the outside at a distance, the idea of preventing others from enjoying the same rights that the included have, with difficulty perhaps, succeeded in obtaining.

Q. Nonetheless, from the time of Hadrian's Wall and the Great Wall of China, walls have always had a very particular role in the history of humanity. The fall of the Berlin Wall in 1989 seemed to have inaugurated a new era: it has assuredly transformed Europe and redefined East-West relations, but the value, indeed, the symbolic value, of walls has in no way been diminished.

A. There are walls under construction in many parts of the world to divide states and peoples, but also quarters of one and the same city: as in Belfast, to separate Catholics and Protestants; as in Padua, where residents had sought in the Via Anelli to protect and separate themselves from neighbors of extra-European origin. If the Berlin Wall was supposed to block off the right of exit of the subjects of communist Germany, these new defensive walls are designed to obstruct the entry of immigrants and of people who are different from the majority or to render their proximity invisible and therefore less intimidating.

Those who raise anti-immigration walls, like the one California has built on the Mexican border, think that they will be able to preserve their privileges large and small if, and for so long as, only they enjoy them. They bring out one of the most flagrant contradictions that afflict our affluent democratic societies: that which sees, on the one hand, a refined culture that shares universalistic and cosmopolitan values and that nonetheless remains the appanage of a minority, often a snobbish one; but that sees, on the other hand, a widely diffused popular culture that, though intoxicated by global consumerism, is terrified by globalization and objectively weak in front of the challenges arising through the opening of borders to cheap labor. The weakest part of our population fears, understandably so, economic uncertainty, and this is primed to foster a fierce attachment to a prosperity that appears increasingly vulnerable, fragile, and temporary. Sometimes, identity politics, religious or otherwise, seems to be a proxy for social and economic distress.

Q. As was described by Marx and Engels in The Communist Manifesto, *the unchecked growth of a financial and economic global power is accompanied by resistances at a local level.*

A. New nationalisms do in fact arise, racism and homophobia spread, violence against women is exacerbated (in Italy, the latter is a frightening phenomenon that has induced opinion makers and women's associations to coin a new term, "feminicide," or crimes committed specifically against women), and a nostalgia for communities of sentiment such as churches or local traditions springs up. And faced with these often aggravated forms of distress, the weakest in society find themselves allied with small and medium local firms, because the global market looks to them all like a wild beast against which no remedy is forthcoming save the old strategies, like a police state mobilized against the "invaders" or anyone who looks different, and protectionist closure by erecting physical barriers.

In this context, the working class seems to be an anachronism. Not because there are no longer inequalities of power or diverging social interests, not because there are no longer classes, but because these inequalities are now represented and expressed in moral and cultural, or even apocalyptic, terms: they are a question of ill luck, of biblical migrations, of financial scenarios perennially at risk of collapse. Yet, when the working class vaunts the legitimacy of the rights it has already won and that are written into statute law, it is accused of "corporativism" or a caste-like egoism, as if respect for social rights that workers enjoyed were indeed equivalent to a call for the protection of privileges, as if the employed bore on their shoulders the responsibility for the lack of work, as if, above all, scarcity of employment depended on the fact of work being regulated and subjected to checks (of the one offering work) and corresponded to rights (of the one who seeks work and does it).

In this panorama, the language of politics and of the universalism of rights is made to seem misguided, ineffectual, and out of place. Yet public reason and political language—namely citizenship in its democratic meaning—are all we have to govern our societies in order to limit the causes of suffering and to offer everyone the possibility of living a dignified life.

Q. *Alongside the erecting of new walls, we also witness the phenomenon of gated communities, which began in the United States and now has proselytes all over the world, from Argentina, where they are called* barrios privados, *to Brazil* (condomínio fechado), *and even to China. In his book* Fortress America, *Edward Blakeley has defined them as "residential areas with restricted access to controls and [where] public space is privatized." They are for the most part surrounded by fencing or barbed wire and patrolled by hired guards who will only admit the owners and their guests. Around ten million Americans are estimated to live in this fashion.*

A. Perhaps gated communities are not directly linked to the need for security, even if that was their justification when they first appeared around thirty years ago. Instead they have been devised and built in order to enable some to live apart from the others, in order not to be contaminated by "the different," and, far more crudely, to underline the wish to have nothing to do with the world of the "not-equal equals," that is, with persons differing in their class, religion, or skin color that the law made equal. Gated communities are a pioneering example of the secession of the few from the "wider" society, anticipating one of the most striking aspects of the oligarchical mutation that we are today experiencing in every Western country and about which I propose we speak at greater length in the course of our conversation: the fact that the "few" no longer want to share with the others the costs of the economic crisis nor to live alongside the "many."

Q. Gated communities resemble small medieval cities protected by walls. Seen from the inside they seem like democratic communities because their members relate to one another socially as "equals": similar incomes (a condition imposed upon anyone seeking to enter), almost always the same race, a similar age bracket. But this equality in remuneration and in power (all the members who are adults and have leases sit on the community's management committee) is applied after a selection that establishes who is to be admitted and who not.

A. If we wished to use classical models, we could say that these communities follow the Spartan model, in the sense that their members are like the citizens of that ancient Greek city, free because and inasmuch as they are socially or ethnically equal. Liberty here comes to be associated with sameness. It is a model of inclusion/exclusion on social grounds also encountered in other contexts. In analyzing it I propose we pay attention to two aspects: first of all, the "modernity" of the phenomenon, which it would be misleading to confuse with a feudal throwback, notwithstanding the fascination with the premodern that so beguiles the critics of modernity (and despite the architectonic similarity, since gated communities boast simulacra of moats and walls, fences and stockades). The second aspect concerns a more complex articulation of democratic forms, manifest precisely in the segmentation of the community.

Q. Let us take things one step at a time: what do you mean by the "modernity" of some of these phenomena, which at first glance would seem to be a return to the ancient?

A. The example of the social policies of the Italian Northern League is highly instructive here. They are not policies that seek to demolish the welfare state where the Northern League is in power: certainly, they do not rule out recalibrating services, but they promise good schools to the children of their "own people," decent accommodation, liveable cities, and efficient healthcare (even to "their" immigrant workers, if integrated into the system and a functioning part of the territory's economy). It therefore sets out to offer social guarantees to its own people while at the same time stipulating who is to benefit from them: perhaps only those who express themselves in dialect, for example. It almost seems to be an attempt, of a wholly unconstitutional kind, to confine social security to those who are equals in some specific sense. And here we see replicated the attempt to build a gated community in one part of the country in the name of the equality and liberty of "members" and not any longer that of citizens. I propose to call this "appropriation of rights": we are in fact concerned here with a shift in perspective that transcends party ideologies; there was an important early manifestation of this phenomenon in Bologna.

Q. *In Bologna?*

A. Yes, in the city that, before fascism, was a pioneer in creating municipal socialism and then in constructing, after World War II, a democratic dispensation with generous welfare provisions and a highly ✓ articulated civil society that promoted participation. Indeed, this was a socialist and communist municipal government certainly very far removed from the ideology of the Northern League. The first time that this change became evident was in 1999, when Giorgio Guazzaloca, the mayoral candidate for the Center-Right, defeated the Left. It was a historic victory and an equally historic defeat, not only because of the abrupt changing of the guard but also because of the deep and highly meaningful causes of it.

Even if what I say may seem a heresy, the Guazzaloca phenomenon was an extreme expression of social-democratic governance rather than an overturning of it. It did not express a call for subversion from the Right or recourse to a free-market dismantling of the regional model of the welfare state (the so-called Emilian model). It represented, rather, a conservative revision of that same model with a view to recalibrating it.

Immigrants were becoming visible, although they were not as yet numerous. University students, no longer politicized, were more and more seen as a disruptive element in the life of the city: the phenomenon of rowdy nights and of the Bolognese gutter punks was just beginning. The city craved the restoration of order that Guazzaloca's mayoral campaign promised.

Q. *Is it not somewhat fanciful to maintain that "Bolognese" social democracy produced the Guazzaloca phenomenon of its own accord?*

A. Like the local elected administrators of the Northern League in the Veneto region, Guazzaloca systematically flaunted the concept of "good government." He even went so far as to say that he took his inspiration from the communist Giuseppe Dozza, the founder of social democracy in Bologna, first mayor after the liberation from Nazism-Fascism, and a member of the Constitutional Assembly. And he insisted above all else on the "nonpolitical" character of his politics: good administration was a liberation from politics and the expression of a *bolognesità* that seemed to be an objective datum, devoid of ideology, identical for all: the attribute of a shared "we," the name of a "good" tradition, and, above all, composed of many elements stemming from the social-democratic mentality. The latter, it should not be forgotten, has a significant bureaucratic core and can therefore engender, if not closely scrutinized from within by liberal criticism and political participation, conservative and even antipolitical (as bureaucratic and regulatory administration) visions of "good government."

The equal distribution of resources and services needs to be translated into criteria, rules, and procedures and then requires the administrative apparatus of the state or, in this case, of the municipal government. Social-democratic politics is nurtured by administration. In this sense, I maintain that Guazzaloca represented the extreme but not reversed image of social-democratic good government. The myth of good administration, as policy makers know, is best rendered concrete when politics is done to one side—the parties retire in good order, and partisan bias yields to the decisions of the "competent," the social analysts and experts in social policy. And this becomes its ultimate conclusion: the negation of politics through good administration.

Q. What implications can the spread of the model of gated communities have for the traditional concept of democracy?

A. There is nothing wrong with a democratic country placing its trust in pluralistic approaches to the administration of some goods at the local level. Uniformizing democracy "in the singular" is not the best paradigm for governing modern society, nor is it for those who see democracy as the political order in which individual liberty is best guaranteed because procedures and rules have the power both to enhance representation and control those who are in charge of power. A democracy composed of atomistic or dissociated individuals risks, as Tocqueville foresaw, disempowering its citizens. Of course, democracy exists in various forms, starting with the one realized in the United States, where citizens can live as separate-and-different but only because they are, and wish to remain, equal before the law and as citizens, where therefore there can be social privileges without their being translated— although this is increasingly difficult—into political privileges. This is the federal model, which heeds liberty more than it does equality.

Michael Walzer has clearly explained how the equality of citizenship functions within countries that are familiar with all the pluralistic effects to be found in cultures, religions, and traditions. And he has distinguished between two forms of democratic republic: the first is the kind that has been consolidated in the United States and that is articulated in hyphenated identities (Italian-American, Jewish-American citizens, and so on): whereby cultural belonging is on the left of the hyphen and political belonging is on the right.

The second form of democratic republic is exemplified by France and is based on the fusion of cultural identity and political identity, where, in other words, democratic citizenship is built up by starting from a nation of those who are equals in something: democracy in the European states in fact issued from a single trunk, that of the nation or national sovereignty. In this second model, which for brevity's sake we will call "continental," constitutional rights have the function, to a still greater degree than in the other model, of limiting the power of the majority, which otherwise would be immense, if not indeed absolute.

The continental model was forged by transferring the principle of absolute sovereignty from the monarch to the people and then to the nation: rights were conceived, on the one hand, as an emanation of the sovereign constituent will and, on the other hand, as a never-secure limit to this will, inasmuch as it is itself rooted in the will of the sovereign people.

Q. Can you give a fuller explanation of this concept, given that in the continental model the defense of rights appears to be always at risk?

A. It is at risk because the basis of citizenship is not only juridical but also cultural and even ethical: here rights, needed by the minorities in order to contain the already excessive power of the majority, contest the equality of the equals. If in the United States rights have from the start had the function of safeguarding the individual against the power of the state and enhancing the broader spectrum of freedom of choice, in the continental model they have been also a means to protect minorities from the uniformity of power that the nation represents. The "majoritarian" temptation is much stronger in Europe, where democracy has decked itself in the garb of the nation: of a "we" that has not been freed of identitary and ethical meanings and that is not only political, although it aspires to be so (one may say that the tension animating continental democracy springs from this permanent endeavor to keep the political separate from and hierarchically imposed on the pre- or nonpolitical, be it social, cultural, or religious). Being Ghanaian-Italian is still something that cannot be understood or proposed, since being an Italian citizen is in fact associated with an identity that goes beyond political citizenship and is very robust, certainly cultural, also religious, and at any event preexisting the construction of democracy, not a product of it.

Given that these pluralist tendencies are less and less of an exception, we should ask ourselves whether it may be necessary to revise the way in which we interpret our democratic tradition so that it does not only signify equality of consideration before the law or by law but also signifies the opportunity for each person to receive equal respect in his or her mode of being, which more and more often is different from that of the majority.

Q. And how in your opinion should we respond to this conceptual challenge to democracy?

A. With an awareness that the existing mutation has torn up the ideological and philosophical roots of democracy, which derive from the Enlightenment. The latter taught us that persons are equal before the state and the law but also that the state must be organized—and limited in its powers—with the aim of permitting each to follow his own destiny according to his own capacities. In the processes now underway, the individual has apparently ceased to be the reference point in relation to which we judge the political community, its place being taken by persons situated in specific religious, cultural, or social contexts.

Q. We will speak at greater length about the causes of the "mutation." But a question immediately arises regarding the impact initially of the decline and then of the disappearance of the Soviet Union, the demolition, symbolic as well as real, of the Wall between East and West, and the absence in the contemporary world of an ideological reference point for the struggle for equality.

A. This was a point much emphasized by Bobbio and raised at the very start of our conversation. Yes, the Soviet Union no longer exists and is reduced to being no more than a chapter in the history books, but we have not therefore eliminated the problem to which the USSR was often seen, mistakenly, as an ideal solution. Our democracies should be capable of producing a politics that voices the call for social justice coming from the citizens without renouncing the universalistic and individualistic foundation of law. There is no need for a totalizing ideology in order to possess and give meaning to the specificities (cultural or otherwise) to which we subscribe in our concrete life.

Q. We must however note the absence of an awareness of these processes, especially in the ranks of the Left, who do not derive any political benefits from them, and at the same time see some of their historical objectives, such as equality, confused with them. Why? How is one to explain it?

A. The traditional Left was born into an ideological order with very clear reference points: they indicated with near certainty where one came from, where one was going, and what forces one could rely upon. But once the Marxist dialectic had crumbled and many of the collective political actors inspired by that doctrine had disappeared, what could the Left link up with? What is its project if in the meantime the very idea of the community of citizens fails and there arises in its place the vision of a society composed of groups that reckon they have nothing in common with the "wider society"? The Left, in short, finds itself in the midst of the decline of the grand ideological narratives and of the overweening rise of the identitary narratives.

Q. Is there in your view any correlation between the processes of rapid globalization in the economic world and the mutation we are discussing?

A. Capitalism has integrated the world and has extended its financial sway, to the detriment of manufacturing and industry (at least in the West). Whereas productive labor and industrial enterprises have an organized physicality that is in no way aleatory, the world of finance has an immaterial character that crosses borders and has no territorial specificity. This seems to push global society in contradictory directions.

On the one hand we are witnessing a process of gradual cultural integration at the global level: in every corner of the planet people listen to the same music, no doubt read the same novels, and develop the same tastes. On the other hand, as if in reaction to this process of depersonalization and disidentification, nationalisms are being reborn, religions regain vigor, xenophobic movements proliferate, identitary forms flare up again. It almost seems as if there is a need to attach ourselves to something ancestral and immutable in order to resist the immateriality of financial power and its transient wealth, which is ubiquitous, global, and the fashioner of consumerist affluence but also of rapid impoverishment.

Q. Had Karl Marx not anticipated these developments?

A. Yes. As we have already said, he was convinced that such tendencies would accelerate precisely in conjunction with the global development of the capitalist economic system. And he criticized the call for national self-determination and democratic nationalism of Giuseppe Mazzini as a rear-guard phenomenon insofar as it tended to discern in the political entity of popular sovereignty the abstract haven in which people would, mistakenly, anchor their liberty. According to Marx, the national-political solution would prove to be transitory because economic organization would unify the fate of the peoples and empty the nation-state, and state sovereignty itself, of any real power and meaning. He thought it would become all the more difficult to establish a definite line of demarcation between one single nation and the others and between these latter and the rest of the world. Global capitalism would unmask the lack of state power, thus showing how theorists and political leaders were wrong in searching for emancipation through citizenship. Marx understood one important negative implication of this fated uniformity, namely that people would turn the ideal of a nation of equal citizens into an identitarian project of nationalism, a myth of sameness, in order to oppose or resist the bewilderment and anomie produced by a global integrated civil society. The political nation would fail while the identitary nation would flourish. In the face of this process of social uniformity, a widespread fear of losing identity is today gaining ground or reawakening. Whatever the validity or otherwise of Marx's explanations, his clear-sighted description of the phenomenon of globalization reflects some of the problems that now afflict us.

2

The Value of Democracy

Q. At the start of our conversation, you related the great mutation to an equally troubling phenomenon, namely, the weariness of democracy. Before addressing this theme, I would like to understand how you came to be involved with these issues. And what was it in your personal and academic background that led you to single out and explore the issue of mutation?

A. My interest is bound up with my intellectual biography. I have always been strongly attracted to politics, independently of my professional life, even before I embarked upon an academic career. I mean here politics as an object of research and study rather than an everyday activity in institutions or movements; I mean it as a public art of reflection, discussion, and reasoning on public issues in the public sphere that is open to all and renders men and women who are foreign to one another capable of associating, creating, and changing opinions and also laws and governments.

I began with philosophy, exploring idealism and the theory of knowledge, in particular the neo-Kantian tradition and positivism. After graduating, I completed a doctorate in social and political sciences at the European University of Florence, moving, through a study of nineteenth-century liberalism, from more narrowly philosophical themes to questions of political theory and the history of political thought. I focused on the work of John Stuart Mill, an author on the margin between theoretical-philosophical and ethico-political reflection, a liberal mind who sought to understand what the role of the intellectual (or, as he put it, of the person of culture) was in a society based on the formation of public opinion and the use of means of information and who finally sketched out a vision of a liberalism alert to social justice and the inclusion of women and the working classes and in the long-term perspective capable of promoting cooperation of producers and consumers as a form of economic system both superior to capitalism and more consistent with a politics based on consent and voting. And working on the diffusion of English liberalism in the age of the Risorgimento, the nineteenth-century ideological and literary movement that helped rouse the national consciousness of the Italian people, I drew closer to democratic thought by way of the study of liberal-socialist authors such as Leonard Trelawny Hobhouse, Edward Bernstein, Carlo Rosselli, and Norberto Bobbio.

Q. *What impact did moving to the United States and spending most of your academic life at Columbia University have upon you?*

A. It has been of crucial importance to my intellectual trajectory, above all because of my encounter with American pragmatism. Before coming to the United States, I had never paid much attention to "thinking-in-a-useful-way" as a functional adjustment of reflection to decision making and problem solving. Nor was it an essential element in the research I was engaged in, although the philosophical thought of Mill explicitly raised questions as to the adjustment of logical models of induction and the generalization of experience and in particular as to the transformation of the criteria of knowledge as a consequence of the preponderance that opinion acquires in societies resting upon a representative government.

When public opinion becomes the engine of government and the perceived legitimacy of the political system of decision making, the forms of reasoning change, as also does the place of specialized knowledge and experts in the resolution of public problems. The pragmatic and democratic approach underpinned my studies: English thought, in the Baconian tradition, and above all American pragmatism, anyway tended in this direction. My acquaintance with pragmatism, in particular the writings of Charles Sanders Pierce, William James, and John Dewey, was however flanked at the beginning by a sense of irritation with the instrumental approach that American thought seemed to me to assume. Under the guidance of a scrupulous professor at the University of Bologna who loved Anglo-American philosophy, Antonio Santucci, I studied texts whose lucidity I greatly admired, although they left me doubtful as to their political implications, which struck me as too concerned with practical results or the beliefs people have respecting their validity. Perhaps the leftist ideal of a well-ordered society situated beyond the here-and-now of our too unjust and imperfect democracies did not help my generation appreciate a philosophical tradition that, as in the case of pragmatism, rejected the dualism between reality and appearance and defined as "reflective thought" any belief or form of knowledge "in the light of the grounds that supported it and the further conclusions to which it tends" (John Dewey, *How We Think* [1933], in *The Later Works, 1925–1953*, 8:118).

American philosophy—as Richard Rorty wrote on several occasions in the course of his lifelong dispute with the European loyalty to dualism between truth and opinion, reality and appearance—is innocent of metaphysics because it resists becoming "caught up in the disastrous appearance/reality distinction." This distinction is disastrous, Rorty explained, because it invites us to neglect, ignore, and even despise our own prosaic lives, and those of our fellow citizens, in the search for a deeper or hierarchically superior unified substance of the truth, according to the illusion that by representing the world in a way that is as much as possible independent of those who inhabit it (of their specificities, needs, and feelings) we would gain in impartial consideration and judgment. And "the view from nowhere" or the "God's eye-view" has been an expression of European pride in making thinking a process of ethereal distance from empirical and concrete living as fatally immersed in "appearance" (Richard Rorty, introduction to John P. Murphy, *Pragmatism: From Peirce to Davidson* [Boulder, Colo.: Westview, 1990], 3–4). Dewey was the philosopher who buried the reality/appearance dualism, or the split between attention to prosaic reflection and the tragic affirmation of truth. Pragmatism is thus the most complete overcoming of any representational approach according to which there is such a thing as deliberation and reasoning that is not the same as thinking about reality as it is, and likewise the view that instrumental thinking is vulgarly utilitarian and in this sense relativist. According to the dualist view, beyond the world we represent to ourselves in order to satisfy our wants or needs, there must be a superior reality that our local thinking is representative of in order for us to escape the fallacy of radical skepticism and relativism. Dewey fiercely opposed this dualism in the name of supreme respect for our ordinary life and resisted the temptation to see "the empirical world in which we live from day to day" as "crass and obdurate, stubbornly un-ideal in character because it is only an appearance of the reality of which thought is the author" (John Dewey, *The Quest for Certainty* [New York: Putnam, 1960], 108). Thus, rather than representations of a substance that make our mind a spectator or the reproduction of an entity that is above us, our mental instruments are beliefs; they are pragmatic guides to action, neither false nor true because they "represent nothing." Beliefs are instead tools and projections that keep action and the out-there reality in indissoluble relation: we do not reason from "nowhere" but from somewhere, in the attempt to proceed somewhere, thus projecting our plans and life ahead. Hypotheses and conjectures are the logical inferences that guide our analysis, both when it is scientific and when it is moral.

Finding myself living in a country in which people believed themselves to be practicing a "democratic way of life" and in which no reflective and theoretical activity disregarded the wider social world, I have learned to value the idea that thought is "useful" and, in this sense, as Dewey maintained, that no form of theoretical thought is ever wholly detached from the world of interests and concrete individual experience. Even analytic philosophy and the theory of knowledge, in other words, even the more abstract forms of thought, contain some direct reference to the world of practical civil and political utility, that is, to what citizens do, propose, wish, and decide.

Q. *Could you elaborate on this point?*

A. Peirce spoke of abduction as a model of logical inference that operates on the world of the hypothetical and the possible rather than on the world of pure and clear ideas to which empirical and sensory reality must adapt. James analyzed the world of habits and interpreted them as second nature that, while making human behavior mechanical, saves energy for the will, which can thus devote itself to more creative endeavors. This pragmatic notion of the autonomy of the ordinary person recognizes that individuals need to rely upon a system of habits that are like guidelines to action: respecting rights, for instance, can become—thanks to education and our daily practice—so imprinted upon our minds as to make us comply with them without consciously planned attention. Habituation to act according to right does not make us less free. This, James thought, is the condition for a society that is able to progress with a minimal use of coercion and in which autonomy can express itself in all practical domains. In the way in which citizens think, they reveal how they relate to others, the prejudices they have, their expectations, the interests that lead them to make specific choices, the emotions that drive actions or control and exalt them. Dewey called this complex world of both political institutions and procedures and interpersonal social relations "democracy." There is nothing mechanical in democracy, he thought, and nothing that proceeds through inertia, although a platform of some ideas is needed in order to make a society democratic not only as a political form of government but also in its social life. We are concerned here with a permanent educative process that "must be born anew in every generation and education is its midwife."

Q. *Those are John Dewey's words.*

A. Yes. In his 1939 text we read:

[Of late] we have had the habit of thinking that . . . democracy is a kind of political mechanism that will work as long as citizens were reasonably faithful in performing political duties . . . we have heard more and more frequently that this is not enough; that democracy is a way of life. . . . But I am not sure that something of the externality of the old idea does not cling to the new and better statement. In any case, we can escape from this external way of thinking only as we realize in thought and act that democracy is a personal way of individual life; that it signifies the possession and continual use of certain attitudes, forming personal character and determining desire and purpose in all the relations of life. Instead of thinking of our own dispositions and habits as accommodated to certain institutions we have to learn to think of the latter as expressions, projections and extensions of habitually dominant personal attitudes.

Dewey was simply renewing and adapting the classical position that maintained that good laws are rooted in customs, a rule particularly indispensable in the case of democracies, in which no authority external to the citizens' will has legitimacy. Dewey: "Because—Aristotle had explained in *The Politics*—there is no usefulness in the most useful laws, even when ratified by the whole body of citizens, if the latter are not habituated to, and educated in the spirit of the constitution."

No thought that is detached, and in this sense "not useful," exists. And democracy, just like the everyday life of its citizens, is necessarily committed to an "interested" thought, a tool for deciding better and for living. "Thinking in the making," which is effectively the motto of pragmatism, means that the rules of logic are fitted to a reason that is experimentalist and will even venture conclusions that may be risky, but only because it knows that they can be changed and corrected. The openness to possibility is never disassociated from the "thinkability" of what we project and plan, in fact the "correctability" of the decisions we make, in our private as well as our political life. The evolution and proliferation of rights in constitutional democracy confirms this view since rights are like the recognition that we may need to change our mind, not only that we choose to change it. Rights regulating abortion, divorce, and same-sex marriage are examples of a society taking into account this changeability in human actions, beliefs, and conventions.

Q. Do you consider yourself to be a pragmatist in philosophy also?

A. Yes. And I am fascinated by a society like the United States, which fosters a sense of individual power and self-esteem in the individual. Some may think that this is simply a fiction, and perhaps it is a fiction, but even if it were, it would not be a pointless fiction. We are under the grip of illusions and fictions; we make decisions taking into account a forecast of events that is itself influenced by illusions, that is, swayed by hopes, fears, preferences, and opinions that derive from an effect of imitation on our part. Edmund S. Morgan wrote in *Inventing the People* (1988) that "fictions are necessary, because we cannot live without them, we often take pains to prevent their collapse by moving facts closer to fit the fiction, by making our world conform more closely to what we want it to be" (14), and in this sense fictions (or functional illusions) take command and reshape our reality. Much like the fiction of popular sovereignty that Morgan reconstructed and explained, the fiction of a self-reliant individual plays a shaping and reconstructive function.

If then by fictions we mean acting under the influence of an "as if" (this is precisely what fiction is), in other words, a norm or regulative ideal that shapes our behaviors and prompts us to act, fictions then become the lymph of action and have a constructive function because they set in motion affective circuits that render us determined, creative, active. The rational use of the emotions, which are irrational forces, is anything but illusory. In this fashion, ideologies become formidable rational forces, visions that cluster around a nucleus of ideas and information, capable of steering collective action in a complex social world, enabling social actors to choose and plan an action for the future, all the while knowing very little or nothing about its chances of success. It is reductive to suppose that politics can be done without ideology, and it is reductive to suppose that ideology is simply an irrational force.

Q. *American society also teaches that fatalism is a sin, perhaps the gravest sin of all.*

A. Because it represses the vital energies and becomes a force of self-censorship and humiliation that, first and foremost, does not penalize only our individual lives but moreover the vision we have of ourselves, the mode in which we perceive ourselves. When the juridical and political foundations recognize, support, and facilitate the self-esteem of persons, the whole society benefits. For democracy is not merely a form of government (although it is first of all a form of government). It is also a way of thinking our relationships with others and above all with ourselves. Saying that we must treat others with dignity and that each person is deserving of respect is, if one thinks carefully about it, a recognition of our own value through the recognition of the value of others.

What is self-belief, and why is it so inimical to fatalism? By way of response, I want to refer to a concrete and personal case. There are words, persons, experiences that mark the lives of each and every one of us. They lodge in our memories, and, like milestones, they punctuate our biographies. Sometimes it is written words, imaginary persons, and narrated experiences that mark our time and much of what we are. In some cases, the impression left by a reading is so strong and clear that it can be precisely dated and specified.

Q. When did this happen to you?

A. In the autumn of 1990. Without overstating the case, I am bound to say that the reading of *Leaves of Grass* by the American poet Walt Whitman marked my soul because it transmitted to me a sense of myself that no other previous reading had done.

> I celebrate myself, and sing myself,
> And what I assume you shall assume,
> For every atom belonging to me as good as belongs to you.
> . . . .
> There was never any more inception than there is now,
> Nor any more youth or age than there is now,
> And will never be any more perfection than there is now,
> Nor any more heaven or hell than there is now.
> . . . .
> Welcome is every organ and attribute of me, and of any man hearty
>   and clean,
> Not an inch nor a particle of an inch is vile, and none shall be less
>   familiar than the rest.
> . . . .
> I believe in you my soul, the other I am must not abase itself to you,
> And you must not be abased to the other.
> . . . .
> And these tend inward to me, and I tend outward to them,
> And such as it is to be of these more or less I am,
> And of these one and all I weave the song of myself.
> I am of old and young, of the foolish as much as the wise,
> Regardless of others, ever regardful of others,
> Maternal as well as paternal, a child as well as a man,
> Stuff'd with the stuff that is coarse and stuff'd with the stuff that
>   is fine,
> One of the Nation of many nations, the smallest the same and the
>   largest the same.

Q. Why do you say that you have been marked by these lines?

A. These lines are evocative and powerful. They led me to ponder the strength that is within us, very often buried under a weight that oppresses us as the heavy burden does the ass: the weight of unchallenge-able authorities that rob us of our speech, humiliate our minds, teach us to be silent or to repeat, convince us that our voices are a nonsaying. I spent a large part of my youth with my heart weighed down by a dumb and solitary struggle between myself and the world, between what I thought and felt and what others thought and felt. How was I to be with others without ceasing to have my own ideas and to be myself? How was I to believe in a cause without becoming dependent upon it and being enslaved to it? How was I to assent without being conformist? When I began to ask myself these questions I was an adolescent who felt the youth movements in which ideally she recognized herself, with their calls for loyalty and with their obligation to be in agreement prior to discussing and understanding, to be too oppressive. The world's voice was always louder, authoritative, and penetrating, and it has not been an easy task to find a balance. Yet, deep down, I did not believe myself to be defeated nor that the context in which by chance I had ended up in was the only context in which I was destined to live. It was possible to choose. Whitman has enabled me to understand this with extraordinary clarity. And above all he has enabled me to see myself. He has taught me to look inside myself for the strength to resist the world with the calm of one who knows that there is only "one" world: the one that we carry within us. It is ours, uniquely ours, whatever our occupation and our language, our age and our gender may be. It does not matter who we are for others and what we are doing: each of us is a universe and the measure of time.

This profound conviction of the value of the single person and of the equality of every human being is the secret force that feeds self-confidence because no authority, no world outside of us, can lay claim to any superiority over what we are. The conscience of the honest man—said Henry David Thoreau—is like a rock upon which the waves of the world break and to which those who withstand them can cling.

Whitman's poems revealed to me what I knew without being aware of it and what lay in a muddled state I know not where in my soul: become what you are, according to the Socratic dictum that inspired the nineteenth-century individualists. Not that there is any obligation to venture upon this work. Nonetheless, amid the myriad duties that entities of every kind impose upon us, we should endeavor to carve out a moral duty toward ourselves: to know our own vocation, to have a strong sense of our own dignity, to be proud of being simply because we are, to not let anyone rob us of this certainty of ours. Is it not this—that is, the putting the world into balance with our own selves—that is in essence the deep reason for our tireless call for justice? Is it perhaps not true that when we cry out at injustice we feel that there is a dissociation between our expectations and what has been presented to us as the only possible choice?

Q. What so far has been the principal field of your research in political philosophy?

A. The theme that has interested me the most and upon which I have concentrated is that of political liberty in contemporary societies: how is it won and sustained, and how may it be lost? What are the institutions through which it is affirmed and consolidated? In this research into the conditions of liberty I have become convinced of the central importance of equality, on the one hand because it renders liberty possible for one and all, and on the other hand because it limits liberty from within, preventing it from turning into privilege, license, and arbitrariness. It is a political liberty in the sense that we enjoy it alongside others—it is not the liberty of the isolated individual—and by means of laws and rules. Finally, it is a liberty granted by the security of law and nurtured by the equal opportunity—which citizenship allows us—to participate in the construction of our own destiny and our society. It is a liberty, in short, that lives in and through communication with others. It is a response, as may be seen, both to atomistic individualism and to the communitarian negation of the individual.

Q. Every European scholar who addresses the history and contradictions of American democracy will inevitably have to deal with Alexis de Tocqueville.

A. When Tocqueville left for America, in 1831, he did not know exactly what he would find there. He came from a society that had overturned a centuries-old system of hierarchies and inequalities but that had not yet arrived at a new order. He therefore set sail from Le Havre in search not of an ideal society but of an interpretative thread that would help him unravel the tangle of events perplexing his country in the aftermath of the French Revolution. In the United States of 1831, he saw the signs of a society different from the French or European, which he called "democratic society." He treated America as an experimental laboratory where the characteristics, the customs, "the spirit" of the new society appeared in all their naturalness. Democracy was no longer the name of a form of government but of a social system.

Q. *How did Tocqueville view the "democratic individual"?*

A. In the course of his journey, he became convinced that America was "one of the countries in the world where philosophy [was] least studied, and where the precepts of Descartes [were] best applied." In other words, in America ideas were mental habits and practices of life rather than abstract principles to be incorporated into codes and imposed through revolutions. There too individualism, like equality, was freed from the potential for revolution that it had in Europe, where, indeed, it had first been theorized by the philosophers and then embraced by political leaders who had imposed it upon society in a Jacobin fashion. Tocqueville had therefore found confirmation of the fact that pragmatic reason was the best ally of social transformations, even the most radical ones, in a society without a center and composed of equals because it favored nonviolent processes of change in modes of thought and therefore in collective behaviors: changes in popular custom, as Antonio Gramsci would later write, that gave ideas and beliefs the time to settle.

Tocqueville thought that individualism in America was not as negative as in France, where it had to combat the hostility of a moral culture that preached subordination and acceptance of one's own destiny (although, being Christian, it professed the gospel of fraternal equality in the name of a single creator). If across the ocean equality was the normal and pacific result of social relations imbued with law and equality of conditions, in old Europe it could become a project of radical leveling that was counterposed to a recalcitrant "caste" reality. In one case, individualism was a question of a "calm feeling," in the other a matter of an envious project of equality pitting the many excluded against the privileged few.

Q. *Tocqueville sought to understand what we too find it hard fully to understand: how it is that equality in modern society is reconciled—if it is reconciled—with the value of the individual.*

A. It seemed to him that in American society, which was neither centralized nor the outcome of a struggle between classes, equality ended up precisely by exalting the individual. It likewise seemed to him that American society, instead of favoring the creation of a mass of identical persons, fostered competition between those who were different. In short, according to Tocqueville, equality in a tempered democracy consisted neither in a communitarian harmony nor in a repressive solidarity whereby the good of the community came before that of its component parts. This elastic relationship between the strength of the individual and equality explains the amazement of those who, like Tocqueville himself, came from a culture in which equality was considered to be a leveling process that rendered everyone identical—by driving all downward—or, to echo Mill, equal like sheep.

Tocqueville was right to observe that Europeans did not know what a society founded upon both the individual and equality was. He was right because a European plurisecular tradition—ideological and political—had suggested something altogether different, that is, that equality means that we are all children of the Creator, but with a double consequence: that we are all equally tainted by original sin, which was a sin of disobedience to authority, and that a supreme authority (the clergy, the saints, the virtuous) should rule us, thus saving us from our equality in sin, from our shortcomings.

Jacobin revolutionary equality, which unleashed the attack on this equality in subjection, was as extreme as the enemy it combated. At any rate, it sought to render all equal in their submission to a republic ruled by the virtuous, by the tyranny of the competent few. Both for the ancien régime and for its gravediggers, it was a heresy to think in terms of the equality of opportunity for individuals to express themselves as best they could. This, however, was what Tocqueville did suggest. This heresy gave birth to America or, if you prefer, to the American myth of which we are all now the sons and daughters. And anyone who has tried it out is bound to feel contented at having known the meaning of equality of opportunity.

When I mentioned "useful thought" and the positive impact it has had upon my own thinking, this was what I meant. And the reference to Whitman likewise tended in this direction: pragmatism is in fact a way of seeing and of living that is adapted to a society founded upon individual responsibility, reciprocity, and a proud sense of being equals in moral value and in dignity, but that society is also an elastic society open to changes. On these foundations, the individual can step forward as a person ready to try and to experiment, one who needs an open and tolerant society as much she needs the air she breathes.

Q. In the time span covered by your research into liberty and equality we have been witness, as we just said, to several twilights of totalizing ideologies. What has the response of political philosophers to this phenomenon been?

A. In its first phase, it was lived and theorized as an emancipatory process. Hence the tendency to exalt contingent events, as against the metaphysics of the "grand narratives," evident in the postmodern philosophies of the 1990s. Thus, a waning interest in the totalizing ideologies and a readiness to accept the contingent without fear at the prospect of failing to give a collective meaning to our individual choices have been hailed by philosophers as marking a passage to adulthood and an end to "beautiful lies." Democratic individuals are used to thinking of themselves as autonomous persons who associate and part company for the most disparate reasons, and in such a way that individual interest and social well-being can intersect (which does not exclude their clashing and moving apart) without an intellectual avant-garde pointing the way or a providential ideology sanctioning objective ties between the individual decisions and the course that History selects and imposes.

We have therefore become a society of individuals yet still a society, not a congeries of atoms. Tocqueville had seen this individual-social network unfurl in American cities and villages through the sole power of individual rights and republican institutions, a network that created an order similar to that of the Newtonian universe, where bodies are held together through the action exercised by their specific weight, each of them being different and productive of a different motion yet conducive to the total order.

If in the premodern epoch philosophers and scientists, in an attempt to explain this order, devised fantastical systems of forces and actions directed by the divinity, after Copernicus, Galileo, and Kepler it seemed that geometrical signs and mathematical calculations, that is, mechanical explanations of the relationships between forces and masses of various sizes, would suffice: an order that proceeded independently by virtue of an immanent motion.

Q. It is the equivalent of what, in a striking phrase, the sociologist Daniel Bell called "the end of ideology."

A. It is not correct to say that there are no longer any ideologies. In a democratic society, they assume the form of reasons that are exchanged: public justifications on the part of whoever is proposing them, but above all without excluding the possibility of the reasons of others becoming ours also tomorrow. In this "free market of ideas"—a phrase originally used by Mill—totalizing ideologies, which are not interested in the exchange of opinions but only in the creation of followers and proselytes, have been set aside.

In coining the expression "the end of ideology," Bell seemed to have forgotten the Millian distinction between "dead dogmas" and "living truths": in a democratic society it is not the ideologies that end but rather the dogmatic form of reasons and judgments, of ideal representations and of justifications. This does not mean that politics expels emotion from our choices. Emotions and passions continue to be the forces that drive us to act for or against: the "end of ideology" does not alter this circumstance. On the other hand, the void created by the exhaustion of the totalizing forms of ideology is hard to deny. The transformation of the dogmatic mentality into a mentality open to dialogue is a process that is complex, difficult, and in no sense mechanical.

Q. Can you be more specific: what impact has the void created by "the end of ideology" had upon political philosophy?

A. Politics needs ideologies, if by ideologies we mean beliefs and visions robust enough to guide us in our interpretation of the fundamental principles that constitutions have adopted, to enable us to bear our disappointment at our political defeats, which need nonetheless to be taken into account, to distinguish ourselves from the others in electoral choices and social alliances, to enable us to justify our choices and to understand fully the difference between those who win majority consent and those who lose it. We can define democratic society as a politically secularized, but at the same an ideological, society informed by a diversity of visions and perspectives and in no wise homogeneous.

In the wake of Quentin Skinner, I use the term "ideology" to indicate the use of beliefs and principles serving to legitimize, and above all to motivate, political behavior; in short, it refers to the active function of political ideas in the interpretation of social facts and interests and in the proposing of social conceptions and actions. The idea of liberty and the idea of equality perform this role in so far as they constitute the shared criteria in relation to which citizens judge their representatives and their policies, criticize the asymmetries of power existing in society, and, finally, mold their political language, associate with one another, and formulate their demands. The "ideological" function of political judgment is the paradigm with respect to which ideas acquire value in the representative system, transcending the limits of the ontology of the will and of the direct and physical presence of citizens in the decision-making process. And if, taking up again the thread of our dialogue, we speak of "mutation" instead of transition or transformation, it is to describe and understand something that alters with regard not to a written plot in a "grand narrative" but rather to a nucleus of ideas that we already have, as a political community, and that for example are reflected in a constitution.

In choosing the term "mutation," we demonstrate that we have taken to heart the death of the totalizing ideologies. The reference point in relation to which we sift reality and describe the mutations in it is not ahead of us, in a future upon which we should project ourselves for reasons that do not depend upon our will, but it is "inside us," so to speak, or in the society that we have ourselves created. It is in relation to that promise of living together in a democratic fashion that I propose to analyze the mutation now underway—beginning with the principles of the equal dignity of the person and equal political liberty that democracy is supposed to guarantee to all of us.

Q. *Do you not reckon that hitherto our societies have sought to develop in a manner consistent with these values?*

A. At least from the French Revolution onward the idea of equal liberty has been our pole star. The journey has been interrupted various times, and in one case, that of Nazism and Fascism, with criminal violence. Western societies have come to believe that the equal distribution of civil and political rights renders us free, without obliging us to conceal or suppress our differences. We have learned that it is possible to be free without having to be identical. Perhaps we have yet to grasp fully that diversity is a value on condition that it not be claimed at the expense of inequality in the distribution of political power and that it not be a cause of prejudice and discrimination.

If during the first half of the twentieth century we understood just how devastating the dream of rendering only the equal free in some specific quality can be, in the present phase we should endeavor to complete that learning process. Our task is, in other words, to place a limit upon the reasons for difference (the difference that the enjoyment of civil rights recognizes) once it lays claim to a special status for itself or seeks to break up the universality of rights in order to erect palisades. The adoption of "juridical pluralism," of the sort that radical multiculturalism—through its advocacy of separated enclaves safeguarding cultural or religious identities—tends to espouse, would be equivalent to the dismembering of the juridical unity of democratic states with a view to promoting the compartmentalization of persons in the separate niches to which they belong: as if each of us were caged in a tradition or in a culture and had as our moral objective the reproduction of that tradition and of that culture.

Whereas in the totalitarian regimes individual liberty was under threat, in the established democracies it is equality and universalism that are in jeopardy. And while liberty has often been won through wars and revolutions that have radically altered authoritarian regimes, this new mutation is internal to the democracies and is subterranean, often silent and invisible, enacted moreover—and in a highly insidious fashion—in the name of respect for the person.

Q. You have also dealt in your writings with some "turning points" in the theory of democracy that are relevant to the processes of mutation that we are analyzing here. I refer in particular to the "liquid" character of democracy and to the debate surrounding the various "souls" of representative democracy. Could you summarize your position on this?

A. Democracy is not good on account of the decisions it enables us to reach. Majority decisions are not always—and not necessarily—the best or the wisest, even when consistent with constitutionalized rights. Democracy is good, rather, on account of its procedures, rules, and institutions; on account of a process that is so constructed as to render all decisions open to criticism and to revision and, above all, to enable whoever should so wish to take part in this process. It is a matter of a work of permanent correction, founded upon the pragmatic idea that imperfections and limits pertain to all human beings without exception and that the learning process advances by trial and error and with the aid of others. Democracy is a political system best characterized as a site of fallibility and mutability. Which is precisely why freedom of speech and the free expression of dissent, along with participation in the process of deliberation in a direct political form (or in the guise of voting), are essential to democracy, inasmuch as they enable one to reassess through cooperation the limits of single individuals.

The dictum *errare umanum est,* which is ordinarily understood to be an invitation to tolerance on account of the possibility of error, can thus be reinterpreted as an admission that making mistakes is a *faculty*—I would be inclined to say a privilege—exclusive to humans. As Albert O. Hirschman has suggested, the dictum should be taken to mean that "only men err." The existence of an error-making faculty is a sign of our liberty to choose and of our consequent responsibility, as well as of the need for cooperation and of its utility.

Q. On the other hand, how do you see the link between elections and representative democracy?

A. Since the advent of representative institutions in the seventeenth century and the constitutional revolutions of the eighteenth century, political theory has divided into two camps. Some thinkers, starting with Emmanuel-Joseph Sieyès, have seen in elections either a tool for selecting a political class or elite with whom to entrust the institutions or a strategy for extending the criterion of the division of labor to politics. Others, like James Madison—though critical of democracy, which, for him as for his contemporaries, meant direct government by the irrational masses and thus mob rule—have considered it to be a way of giving a voice to interests and hence of channeling the participation of society in the state, avoiding a translation of interests, of the few and the many alike, directly into government.

My own idea is that the traditional dualism between generality and individual interests, from which the modern theory of representation arose, is recast in our society in the form of a dialectic between the "politics of ideas" and the "politics of presence," and representative democracy requires both. In fact, neither of the two models taken in isolation offers an adequate response to the problem of representation, whereas together they define the character of modern democratic society, which describes itself through norms and procedures, but also through ideas and symbolic forms, and at the same time is solicitous of subjects and their interests.

When Anne Phillips and Iris Marion Young called into question the old adage to the effect that women should not regret their absence from politics because they anyway have a strong presence in the social and economic domains, they based their argument upon the complementarity between "interests" and "modes of belonging," between "presence" and "ideas." In essence, visibility or presence in the social sphere cannot be held to compensate for invisibility in representative politics because in a democratic society a political voice cannot be swapped for or interchanged with a social one: those with a prominent role in society do not necessarily escape being the victims of discrimination as political subjects.

Q. Women with brilliant careers can be discriminated against, or offended in their dignity, just as easily as women who do not have a career. Do you think that in democracy citizenship comes before other identities?

A. Yes, because it concerns civil and political liberty and therefore either the safeguarding of interests or the assertion of power and the capacity to make decisions. Liberty from subjection or domination focuses on the *form* or *manner* of decision making, that is, on the *position* of those who are affected by decisions as a result of the overall process. It is not the decision per se that should thus be taken into account but the decision within a context of political relationship. Not to have a political voice guaranteed by a system of rights denotes a plight of formal and actual domination for which no laws, no matter how good they may be, can compensate. As a claim to an equal voice and consideration, political liberty is able unerringly to unmask relations of submission, docility, and complete subordination of some individuals to the will of others.

An exemplary rendering of the coequality relationship between individual liberty and political liberty has been offered by Hans Kelsen in his *General Theory of Law and State* (1945):

The will of the community, in a democracy, is always created through a running discussion between majority and minority, through free consideration of arguments for and against a certain regulation of a subject matter. This discussion takes place not only in Parliament, but also, and foremost, at political meetings, in newspapers, books, and other vehicles of public opinion. A democracy without public opinion is a contradiction in terms. Insofar as public opinion can arise only where intellectual freedom, freedom of speech, press and religion, are guaranteed, democracy coincides with political—though not necessarily economic—liberalism.

In sum, a direct reference to the structure of power reveals the political dimension of liberty from subjection, a primary good in and by itself.

Q. *What consequences follow from this?*

A. Some contemporary studies have investigated the issue of representation as part of political justice or from within the broader analysis of identity politics, group rights, and multiculturalism. They discuss representation with a view to solving deficits of representativity in our advanced pluralist democracies—the visible fact that some portions of the citizenry are underrepresented or proportionally less represented than others. Hence the challenging debate over equal representative opportunity, fair representation, and the search for electoral systems that can render representation more expressive of the identities and claims of the represented.

Yet the criterion of justice in representation is normative in the sense that it is not conditional on the achievement of any specific outcome that the citizens may legitimately seek (for example, reparation for past injustices such as discrimination and exclusion). This criterion consists in the actual and concrete possibility that all citizens should be able to participate voluntarily as well as be heard and have effective advocates of their causes. It supports political minorities not because it favors them or compensates them for being in the minority but because it does not give the majority more than its numerical due. Thus, justice in representation is proportional, not reparative, because it is a claim of quantitative accuracy and thus rigorously consistent with democracy. The achievement of reparative justice may or may not be the outcome of the citizens' political presence. Yet, whatever the outcome, it should certainly not be the reason that justifies justice in representation.

Q. What if, in a hypothetical case, no group of citizens suffers or has suffered discrimination?

A. Representation should still follow the norm of proportionality with the political opinions and partisan views the citizens develop and hold in society. Parity is the criterion, the norm that provides for the democratic legitimacy of majority decision making. This is consistent with democracy, which begins, as Robert Dahl has written in *On Political Equality* (2006), with the "moral judgment that all human beings are of equal intrinsic worth, that no person is intrinsically superior to another, and that the good or interests of each person must be given equal consideration."

The norm of parity that women claimed means that all citizens should have the chance to express their views in order to influence and if need be to repeal existing laws or decisions; moreover, by making their voices heard, minorities remind the majority that it is just one possible majority. This amounts to saying that an election is not just a race but a way of participating in the creation of the representative body—the way citizens "send candidates to the assembly." This nicely captures the distinction within the suffrage between the "right of representation" and the "right of decision" since the equal prospect of success should refer primarily to the possibility of acquiring representation through voting.

Thus the issues of justice raised by representation are issues of the equal chance to have one's voice heard or represented not as a concession or compensation for past or present exclusions but as a means of effective participation here and now in the making of politics. This is why I suggest we call justice in representation *democratic*. Democratic representation is just representation insofar as it involves issues of advocacy and representativity and thus issues of a *meaningful* presence, not simply *a* presence, in the play of discord and agreement that is democracy.

Q. Why do you propose the concept of "representativity"?

A. In order to stress the role of representation as a medium that exalts the specificity of the participants in the electoral race and induces voters to seek out the best candidate, looking for an advocate, not a signpost. In a representative government, most political questions are determined by elected officials whose attitudes upon a variety of issues are public knowledge, while most of their constituents' views remain anonymous and cannot be identified individually. Constituents are generally identified through their representatives; they are identified by reflection. Hence, representativity is essential because it allows the citizens' opinion to be identified and known.

Thus, when voters elect representatives, they tend *not* to elect candidates who differ from them in some important respects. The goal of representation is not merely to designate representatives or mandataries (selecting neutrally competent agents) but to give a "part" of the citizenry a political individuality and in this way create the conditions for political dialectics and friendly partisanship.

It is certainly true that, as Frank R. Ankersmit has argued in 1997, "we can only talk about representation where there is difference—and *not* an identity between the representative and the person represented." Yet it is not the existential presence that should be our parameter of representative relation but presence through ideas. Representatives and represented are certainly not identical, but they can have, and actually should have, some relevant similarity at the level of visions and ideas, a similarity that they construct, transform, or interrupt.

As for the second component of the process of democratic representation, *advocacy*, it casts light on the nature of political deliberation. Far from transcending the specific situation of citizens, deliberative reasoning rests on the premise that specificity needs to be known and acknowledged. Therefore, "understanding" and "hearing" are the faculties at work in deliberative speech just as they are in forensic speech. They express the complex nature of the work of the representative, who should *adhere* to her cause but *not be driven* by it. They allow us to see better the competitive nature of democracy, which relies heavily on personal ability and character. So although every citizen can become a representative in theory and de jure, citizens select those whom they judge to be better advocates. They do not choose randomly or feel it is enough that the candidate belongs to their group (they, in fact, discriminate within their own group), although they do not want someone who holds opposite ideas to their own.

Q. Having clarified the meaning and values of representation, let's go back to two basic questions. Why is women's underrepresentation a problem, or why is it seen as a problem by women to begin with? And why is it important to have women elected to representative institutions even if it does not guarantee any women-friendly decisions?

A. In the last two decades, these two interrelated questions have intersected the issue of "justice in representation" as an issue that challenges advanced democracies almost everywhere, with very few exceptions (for example, in the Scandinavian countries). Anne Phillips in *The Politics of Presence* (1995) has given us good reasons to argue that in order to increase the number of elected women modern democracies should be ready to support legislative initiatives that are not free from contradiction, for example, "quotas." Gender rebalancing within democratic institutions, so the argument goes, would justify a temporary violation of the blind-equality principle, which characterizes the right to suffrage in modern constitutional democracy. Meanwhile, some countries, like France, have tried to go beyond quotas and have tackled this issue by introducing a 50 percent criterion in the composition of party lists (using the state's financial support to political parties as an incentive for enforcing *parité*). Finally, proportional representation has also been used in several countries as a means to correct the underrepresentation of some groups (although not only women) by containing majoritarianism.

Quotas, *parité*, and proportional representation have been, and are, the main strategies for redressing injustice in political representation and amending the underrepresentation of women. These strategies are an altogether explicit recognition of what we said above: representation is a democratic value and moreover a form of participation. The search for strategies of redress is an undoubtedly important fact that testifies to a change in women's (and leftist movements') attitudes toward representative politics. No longer does an ideal of direct participation fuel their mistrust of such strategies. As Jane Mansbridge and Iris Marion Young have argued, in established democracies exclusion may take new forms—one of them is precisely depriving citizens of an equal chance to be represented. Thus in representative democracy nonrepresentation—that is, lack of advocacy and representativity—is the most radical form of disenfranchisement.

I would thus argue that the demand for representation is a means of defending interests and at the same time a value not wholly reducible to interests, namely, the universality of citizenship. It is a question of political liberty: women wish to participate in the political contest in the guise of citizens who enjoy equality in terms of power. They wish the procedures and the rules to be framed so as not to exclude those who do not belong to the male population. For this reason, a gratifying social identity, even one that is important in terms of economic influence, cannot compensate for a weak political identity. Having a career is no recompense for not having a presence within elected institutions (although enjoying an equal right to vote).

The consequence is that the mix of a "politics of presence" and a "politics of ideas" produces a virtuous intertwining between a conception of representation that is based upon interests and one that considers representation to be an expression of political liberty: where the former is concentrated upon specific aspects, the latter asserts the generic character of citizenship and is blind to social particularities. Having the "politics of ideas" interact with the "politics of presence" obeys a logic that has linked civil rights to social rights: the former, precisely on account of their being enjoyed as rights and not as privileges, must be distributed in an absolutely equal fashion, while the latter, on account of their having a real effect, must be solicitous of social differences or of specificities of culture, of gender or of an economic nature.

Q. Based on these theoretical premises, why do you think that the case of women exemplifies an important aspect of the mutation of democracy?

A. My argument on women and political citizenship in stable democracies revolves around two correlated phenomena: women's quest for presence in representative institutions grew hand in hand with (a) the decline of the role of political parties and (b) the decline of a relationship of trust between political parties and their electors (a decline that became dramatic in Europe with the end of the Cold War).

One might say that the decline of the political parties (the decline of "party democracy," according to Bernard Manin) translated into an increasingly urgent quest on the part of women for a presence in politics. A few years before the victory of Tony Blair's Labour Party in 1997, Anne Phillips had rendered this inverted relation as one between "politics of ideas" and "politics of presence." In her struggle for a rebalancing of women's presence on Labour Party lists, Phillips argued that the "politics of ideas" (namely, party identification) was no longer enough to make women feel represented. The quest for quotas, a phenomenon that has become widespread throughout Europe in recent decades, was in and by itself a denunciation of a lack of women's presence within elected institutions following the decline of trust in political party. Since ideas were no longer able to convey citizens' social presence, women had to find other ways to make themselves visible and more precisely to make their ideas and interests heard.

Q. *Let us try to clarify what was meant by the "politics of ideas" in order to make sense of the quest for a "politics of presence."*

A. The centrality of the "politics of ideas" corresponded to an age in which political parties enjoyed strong legitimacy among their members and, more in general, among citizens. They belonged to an age in which democratic citizenship was consolidated through party identification. Parties were the medium for both presence and ideas. As a matter of fact, when women's claims for presence started in the 1980s, political parties were already using quotas to allocate "presence" proportionally among the social, economic, and cultural groups they included or represented. For instance, in the case of Italy's Christian Democratic Party, Italian Socialist Party, and Italian Communist Party, their national governing bodies were filled in proportion to the weight of the groups they comprised (blue- and white-collar workers, farmers, professionals, women, students). It is impossible to establish a direct causal correlation between the parties' de facto quota systems and the content of their electoral programs. Yet, proportionality and quotas were adopted to bolster militants' belief that their party was an inclusive universe and that they had a voice in it. The stronger their belief in their party's representative power, the more the "politics of ideas" preempted any need to vindicate their "presence." Which means that their vindication of "presence" followed the decline in party loyalty: this was one important meaning of the quest for quotas. Women's claim for a political "presence" brought to the fore the crisis of political party in contemporary democracies. Representation has lost advocacy because political parties had lost their representative appeal among electors. To return to what we said above, the loss of advocacy has followed the decline in representativity by political parties by dint of a process of political secularization that has swept away ideological creeds.

For at least three decades after World War II, the "politics of ideas" was able to satisfy representativity. Just to limit myself to the Italian case, it is certain that crucial reforms that were passed in the 1970s (from the law establishing the right to divorce to that regulating the voluntary interruption of pregnancy) were a direct expression of the success of "politics of ideas," not "politics of presence." Political parties were very much to the fore in vindicating those rights. For sure, social movements, and the women's movement in particular, played a crucial role in making political parties more determined and resolute in pursuing that politics and winning broad consent in society at large and in legislative assemblies. Yet the strong influence that those movements had on parties was not measurable in terms of their "presence" in the lawmaking bodies.

As a matter of fact, the number of women within the Italian Parliament and the upper echelons of political parties was not notably higher than it is today. Yet parties were able to represent and implement political programs that women could identify with (and actually did). "Politics of ideas" was then perceived by the citizens as in near perfect harmony with "politics of presence" (construed as a politics that was alert to the "'interests" of the citizens). Political scientists have argued that this phenomenon of alignment of ideas and presence in European postwar democracies was attributable to the high degree of social and cultural homogeneity evident within political parties and society as well. Homogeneity in class interests made "politics of ideas" the equivalent of a politics of identity insofar as citizens identified themselves with their ideological loyalties.

Thus, one might be tempted to hazard the following conclusion: the "politics of presence" acquired salience as ideological unification went into decline. It emerged when the pluralism of interests and identities became more fragmented and pronounced and when groups referring to a party realized that their ideological loyalty did not satisfy their requests but actually translated into a sacrifice of their requests. The communication between civil society and political society—between movements and political parties—was an essential factor in the success of the "politics of ideas." It was also the expression of the democratic nature that representation acquired thanks to political parties.

Q. Does this mean that so long as the "politics of ideas" worked, the "politics of presence" was not necessary? Does democracy work best when the homogeneity of interests and ideas is at its height?

A. Let us go back to the analysis of the age of democracy of parties. When women started claiming the right to be included in party lists, when they contested the way party lists were drawn up, they showed they no longer thought it was crucial to follow the "party line" in order to win their cause. In fact, they thought it was important to be able to disobey the party line and declare openly that the "politics of ideas" was no longer representative of *their* interests or "ideas." If women were not able to "disobey" the party, to betray their ideological loyalty, they would not ask for a "politics of presence." But women became able to disobey and to be disloyal—and their decision was not a minor one; in fact it was a tremendously important decision that questioned the way in which representation was performed and managed.

If women needed to disobey their party—and ask for more presence—it was because the politics they gave priority to was no longer identical with the politics their parties selected as prior. Anne Phillips made this point in an essay translated into Italian in 2000 ("Perchè é importante se i nostri rappresentati sono donne o uomini?" *Info/Quaderni* 6, no. 7–9 [2000]: 133–144). The priority of "presence" over "ideas" indicated a break in the unity of representation as it was built up during the age of party democracy. When women called for a greater presence on party lists or within elected institutions, it was because they no longer trusted their party; they did not believe that the "politics of ideas" was capable of representing their absence (or lack of presence). They no longer believed that their absence from decision-making institutions was irrelevant to the fulfillment of their demands. They no longer had any faith in the advocacy offered by parties. They no longer believed that the politics of ideas was a substitute for "direct" presence, nor did they think that it rendered the latter nugatory. The simple fact of being present acquired salience. Thus, the rise of a politics of presence signaled a crisis of representation, betokening as it did a crisis of representativity in the matter of political affiliation, that is to say, in the institutions (parties) that were supposed to do the work of advocacy and transform electoral into representative democracy.

3

The Decline of Universalism

Q. You locate the great mutation in the context of the decline of universalism. The idea that human beings, by virtue of sharing the same destiny on this earth, have in common the same condition of finitude dates back to antiquity. There are traces of it even in Cicero. Can you rehearse the journey of universalism in Western philosophy?

A. Briefly said, universalism as a moral philosophy has classical, Hellenistic, and Christian origins. In the *Republic* Cicero speaks of a human nature endowed with a capacity to formulate moral judgments and to apprehend the meaning of justice, and having beforehand the same ability to feel pain. In the Sermon on the Mount, Jesus speaks of a common human condition of suffering, succor, and forgiveness: natural sentiments that bring us closer to those who are distant from us, from our world, from our affects and concerns. In humanist and then in modern philosophy these ideas converge in the image of society as concord-discord, a vision that posits, beyond differences, a common sympathy between human beings and all creatures that allows for communication (and sometimes conflict). In the Hellenistic tradition, both the Stoic and Epicurean, which inspired humanism and, subsequently, the philosophy of the seventeenth-century French moralists from Blaise Pascal to Michel de Montaigne, we find a conception of the human world that rests on a double nature: a universal one, which corresponds to the minimal capacity to have primary feelings and to

63

formulate some moral judgments, and a particular one, linked to the world of beliefs, customs, and institutions, which societies create and which, by dint of their persistence through time, come to seem natural.

This universalist vision is given a more systematic form by the Enlightenment, both the Scottish and French. Yet eighteenth-century philosophy is not monolithic, nor is the Enlightenment, a term deployed by Kant in the 1790s to refer to a late synthesis of ideas elaborated upon earlier by a wide range of different philosophers. The writings of David Hume, Adam Smith, Jean-Jacques Rousseau, and Immanuel Kant, or even of the "contextualist" Edmund Burke, speak to us of human beings as a species that—either through natural feeling and sensations, or because endowed with forms and schemes of reasoning that structure inferences and transcend specific knowledge, or because of their innate love for freedom—is able to communicate, search for agreement, and forge pacts of union among themselves despite the profound differences consolidated through processes of historical and cultural sedimentation. It is not necessary to interpret universalism as a moral absolute that speaks the language of abstract duty in order to appreciate these insights. Rousseau posited the existence of a basic sentiment of self-survival and compassion for other beings as natural feelings, prior to reflection and intellectual elaboration, that belong to the species and its members. One can view it as a vehicle for communication and the critical examination of existing institutions and social relations: a shared feeling that enables us to achieve a condition of primary understanding even if, owing to our differences in language and culture, we fail to reach a full understanding. Yet it is not unison as perfect concord of mind that these philosophers proposed when criticizing divisions between classes and groups or wars and domination. Kant's *Project for a Perpetual Peace* represents a bold juridical and moral translation of this tradition of thought, one that has retained all its relevance.

Q. *Justifying individual liberty and its realization in the state of right.*

A. Yes. From the idea of a divided human nature at once social and asocial, Kant comes to recognize our propensity to live in society and at the same time to transcend it, whether when we aspire to form our own moral autonomy or when for the most disparate reasons we cross the bounds of the state and of our own culture. The positive tension between social and individual is reflected in the idea of "cosmopolitan right": a prerogative of liberty in the guise of the security of life and of respect for the person, which Kant assigns to every individual and which constitutional states are better disposed to and, thus, must recognize and respect. In the idea of cosmopolitan right we see reflected our universal condition as individuals who must operate in and create their own world (which may mean traveling or moving and communicating with strangers) but also as individuals who live and are raised in diverse cultures and different places. From this condition, which is ingrained in our nature as humans, who do not rely upon instincts for their survival but upon their choices, the risk of mistreatment and discrimination may arise. And cosmopolitan right therefore does not protect abstract individuals but persons who are concretely diverse—and also "visibly" diverse and foreign to others.

In proclaiming the priority of individual rights, cosmopolitanism has its most natural abode in the sphere of justice; it aspires to subject politics to morality and right through the transformation of political power from the arbitrary expression of the will of the strongest and the mighty to a legitimate use through the law and a process of decision making that is public and thus exposed to the judgment of the subjects themselves. To adapt this idea to our society, we might say that the better arbiters, in this context, are courts of justice rather than parliaments or the executive branch of government. According to Kant, cosmopolitan civil rights do not belong to the sphere of the good (morality) or of power (politics). Indeed, they do not pertain to philanthropy, and they only concern politics insofar as justice is enforced by constitutional states, which limit their own jurisdiction in such a way as to render the surface of the globe relatively open to persons choosing to move about and to travel, to seek knowledge, and to ensure that their peregrinations do not involve renouncing their specificity, culture, and religion. It is thus their differences that call for a right, and it is their equality as humans that justifies it.

Like the fundamental rights to life, liberty, and property, cosmopolitan civil rights are claimed in the name of a good that is moral: that is to say, the single individual. According to Kant's *Perpetual Peace*, it is a matter "of the right to present themselves to society [as belonging] to all mankind in virtue of our common right of possession on the surface of the earth."

These rights are conceived as a claim against the constituted authority: they are not "political rights" since they do not assign to individuals the power of the vote in and on public questions. In order for them to be respected, it is necessary for every state to incorporate them into their codes, turning them into articles of positive public right and thus to limit their decision-making power on issues pertaining to freedom of movement and hospitality. This can enable foreign individuals to claim them and, where necessary, to appeal to the courts in order to safeguard them. Just as in the case of the declaration of rights within the national constitutions, cosmopolitan civil right is a limitation upon political power. It is therefore respected on condition that governments themselves become limited or constitutional.

The Kantian model of perpetual peace has a "negative" character in the sense that its justification is so constructed as to prevent states from exercising their sovereignty against individual rights; the model does not preach a new order or call upon a political will to establish a global government. If Kant did not propose a world government it is because his goal was not to transcend states but to prove how they would in the long term cooperate and therefore accept restrictions upon their power and constitutionalize their conduct not only toward their own subjects but as regards all individuals. Hence his conclusion that if all states were to attain the condition of legitimacy through rights limiting and making power representative of the liberty and equality of all their subjects (that is to say, if all were to become republican or constitutional), they also would be readier to respect cosmopolitan civil rights.

Q. It is easy therefore to understand why for Kant peace was an imperative.

A. The permanent risk of war, according to Kant, is responsible for autocracy and, in particular, for the justification of an increase in force and in policies of emergency that tend almost inexorably to violate liberty and rights in the name of security. In a scenario in which life is threatened and the crisis is radical, the defense of security can justify the adoption of exceptional means in the use of force. *Bios* prevails over *nomos*.

Q. The adoption of emergency legislation on the part of the government of the United States after the terrorist attacks of September 11, 2001, seems to confirm the Kantian paradigm according to which national security is an essential prerequisite of cosmopolitan civil rights.

A. Peace and liberty—Bobbio maintained—stand or fall together. *This* is what I call a universalistic vision. It was not buried with the birth of the nations and romanticism's reaction against the Enlightenment; if anything it has been reformulated in the light of the recognition of the specificity of cultures and nations. In fact, one can speak of a transmutation of individualist cosmopolitanism into a cosmopolitanism of the nations: this twin track of the universalistic ideal is the cultural underpinning of the project of the European Union. The anthropological unity of human beings is an ideal and a value that runs through the writings of the modern thinkers to whom our own liberal and democratic tradition is indebted. It certainly permeates the writings of Smith and Rousseau, who, notwithstanding the differences in their moral philosophies and in their envisioning of a political order, held that societies were legitimate or just if organized so as to be emancipated from the subjection of some to the power of others, also creating the normative conditions for bringing persons and peoples closer or at least turning them into peaceful neighbors.

This is particularly true of Smith, whose opposition to monopolies and whose conviction that the market was destined to emancipate society and individuals from irrational, warmongering, and unjust forms of dominion was born of the promise that the division of labor rendered the specific competences of each more conducive to the general welfare and more prone to coordination. Exchange dictated by interest was thus seen as an engine for the perfecting of minds and societies, bringing even the poorest, those whose livelihood depended upon their labor, to free themselves from being condemned by nature to a life of misery and slavery, to demand higher wages, and finally to organize themselves with a view to giving voice to their own demands. *The Wealth of Nations* contains the first robust formulation of struggle between classes and of the relationship between political and economic power. It is Smith who, before Marx, writes that the holders of capital would use their power and influence to persuade magistrates and governments to defend their interests against those of the wage earners and that the power of the state could be mobilized in the service of the most powerful class.

Society—Rousseau would add—is founded upon conflicting interests, and for this reason equal liberty can be achieved only if individuals agree on an equal distribution of the power to give themselves laws and to do so in such a way that utility encounters justice, or the interest of the individual that of the citizen. In other words, the need to associate and the impossibility of living an independent and isolated life must become for individuals an opportunity to create an artificial order in which each is able to live with equal dignity alongside others, without succumbing to the arbitrary will of anyone but obeying the laws that they themselves help make.

Legal equality, Rousseau again observed, becomes the indispensable precondition, without which liberty remains a privilege of the few, is associated with power, and distances itself from right, shedding the prerequisites of the law and acquiring those of brute force and oppression. Personally, I identify with this ideal of the emancipatory function of politics, from which it is possible to elicit the idea of cosmopolitan right as a project of coordination and even cooperation between peoples, an idea that was not abandoned in the nineteenth century and achieved new life in the twentieth.

Q. How did this perfecting of cosmopolitan right occur? Is it perhaps not the case that the twentieth century was marked by nationalisms?

A. The vision known as cosmopolitanism is a heterogeneous family of ancient lineage, just like universalism, of which it is in practice a variant. Though rooted in liberal political thought and in the individualism of rights, its offshoots are quite various and may be at odds with one another. Its liberal-humanist branch stems from Hellenistic philosophy, in particular from Stoicism and from the modern doctrine of natural rights. Its liberal-economic branch is more recent and is descended from the ideal of the emancipation of civil society from the shackles of feudalism and state absolutism.

Notwithstanding the differences, both these traditions hold that national sovereignty is an obstacle because it interferes with individual choices through the coercive power of the law, restraining, instead of facilitating, exchanges of goods and the free movement of individuals. The nation has erected cultural barriers while state sovereignty, upon which it hinged, has used countless stockades and enclosures to divide up the world. Yet precisely in the wake of the recognition of the principle of self-determination of nations, we have witnessed the rise of a third branch of cosmopolitanism: the one that we may call democratic or political, through which the nation can and should become the vehicle of a new international order.

Q. Why do you call it "democratic cosmopolitanism"?

A. Because it is an offshoot of the regulative idea of a peaceful Europe composed of political nations that are politically autonomous and ruled by constitutional or republican governments. As an idea of peace in diversity and in liberty, the inspiration underlying this cosmopolitanism has been reclaimed from the Enlightenment onward by European intellectuals, heirs of the humanistic ideal of concord that Erasmus of Rotterdam, among others, entertained. It then became a political project that inspired the democratic revolutions of 1848–1849 and finally was renewed after World War II. It has linked Kant's cosmopolitanism of individual rights, the democratic universalism of the Marquis de Condorcet, and, finally, Giuseppe Mazzini's idea of a "law of the peoples." In more recent times, the European Union has sought to realize it, turning our continent into the political laboratory for a postnational order of democratic cooperation based upon rights and upon law, an order that aspires to be an alternative to hegemonic and imperial projects.

Q. I wonder if we might pause for a moment and consider the figure of Mazzini and his role in this debate.

A. He was not only the spiritual father of Italian unity but also the far-sighted theoretician of the self-determination of peoples, the bearer of a message, on the one hand, of popular self-determination and, on the other hand, of the global assembly of free peoples—a vision that embraced the universalistic teaching of the Enlightenment, despite his persistent opposition to eighteenth-century philosophy, which he identified with abstract individualism, the egoism of interests, and utilitarian liberalism. Mazzini was the inspiration, highly respected in his own time, behind the cause of national emancipation from despotic and colonial domination. He was a figure of real international prominence and a leader to whom many nations looked. "Nation stands for equality and democracy," he wrote in 1835, before his exile in London: only on this condition is it "community of thought and destiny." He believed, in the wake of Rousseau, that where a law treating all equally as citizens is lacking there exist neither peoples nor nations but only opposed and hostile castes and thus inequality and oppression. Such a motley assemblage of subjects can at best be a "crowd" of bearers of interests bound by calculations of advantage and utility, without any tie of solidarity. The nation, as Mazzini understood it, is the political antithesis of the aristocratic principle, just as the principle of association is the antithesis of both subjection and atomistic individualism: we may say that the nation as the political association of free and equal citizens is the universal language of humanity, spoken in the language of each people. In sum, Mazzini was an original, if not very systematic, political thinker who framed principled arguments in support of various progressive causes, from universal suffrage and social justice to women's enfranchisement. Perhaps most fundamentally, he argued for a reshaping of the European political order on the basis of two seminal principles: *democracy* and *popular self-determination*.

These claims were extremely radical in his time, when most of continental Europe was still under the rule of hereditary monarchies and multinational empires such as the Habsburgs and the Ottomans. Mazzini worked primarily on people's opinions, in the belief that radical political change first requires cultural and ideological transformations in which to take root. He was one of the first political agitators and public intellectuals in the contemporary sense of the term: not a solitary thinker or militant but rather a political leader who sought popular support and participation. His figure and ideas had an extraordinary appeal for successive generations of progressive nationalists and revolutionary leaders from his times until well into the twentieth century; his life and writings inspired many patriotic movements in Europe, Latin America, and the Middle East, as well as the early Zionists, Gandhi, Nehru, and Sun Yat-Sen.

Q. Do you hold that, out of all the existing descriptions of the nation, the one bequeathed to us by Mazzini is the most promising?

A. I do. It is rich in normative and political implications that transcend the epoch, the personal history, and even the ideology of Mazzini and locate it within the Kantian tradition in a broad sense, notwithstanding his unrelenting critique of eighteenth-century individualism and cosmopolitanism. At any rate we must not forget that Kant and Mazzini shared the republican idea, although they based the republic upon different premises: the former upon normative principles of individual rights and liberty that made the republic identical to the constitution, the latter upon a sovereign collective will that laid claim to self-determination as a condition that lent legitimacy to the constitution. Kant searched in right for the justifications for limiting political power, whereas Mazzini held that without an explicit and active will of the people, neither right nor the constitution were possible. The former tried to avoid the moment of the will in order not to subordinate the achievement of a legitimate order to people's consent and instead relied upon the norm and upon the unpremeditated function of anthropology that drove men to find solutions suited to needs and interests, as if "nature" drew them and not their subjective will; the latter trusted rather in intentional construction organized through consensus achieved by political participation and leadership. Kant and Mazzini bear witness to the two paths, one legalistic and the other voluntaristic, taken by modern republicanism.

Q. Let us return to democratic cosmopolitanism: do you view it as a political response to globalization?

A. By contrast with the liberal-economic version, the idea of democratic cosmopolitanism does not conceive of globalization as a naturally self-regulating phenomenon. As a "regulative idea," democratic cosmopolitanism represents the reluctance of politics to capitulate to the so-called spontaneity of economic competition and to the so-called naturalness of the laws of the market. It reaffirms the power of associated individuals and of peoples to govern their own lives. Thus, despite its adherence to the utopian heritage of perpetual peace, the aspiration to reaffirm the value of politics puts democratic cosmopolitanism midway between the tradition of Kant and that of Rousseau and Hegel. Not because, like Rousseau and Hegel, it opts for the centrality of the sovereign nation-state but because in the eyes of cosmopolites a democratic inspiration such as the liberty of civil society can, if left to itself, become the source and site of new privileges and forms of domination masked by the argument of consent to trade.

An example of canny consent may be the unwillingness of the United States and the European Union to lower their barriers to trade in agricultural goods with developing countries. Of course, these countries are too weak to make their voices heard and their bargaining power effective. What we blithely call agreement in exchange and trade neglects sometimes the fact that partners have to be equal in power in order for the rule of the open market to be legitimate, that is to say, based on voluntary participation and liberty. The premise would be that partners are morally at liberty whether to join or not. Without an equal power to withdraw shared by all the participants in a market enterprise there is no such thing as consenting to exchange and an open global market. The proponents of democratic cosmopolitanism aspire to create a space for political liberty beyond nation-states and a space of rights beyond the economic freedom of trade. They do this in the name of the right to a political voice and not simply in the name of humanity (as in the moral tradition of universalism we have examined earlier); they advocate thus the creation of political and juridical institutions capable of governing global civil society and of curbing the authority of states when necessary. Contemporary scholars avowedly committed to this project, from Daniele Archibugi to Étienne Balibar, though they take different stances, are all seeking to devise a charter of citizenship, that is to say, one that is not rooted solely in the state or in a specific juridical space but belongs to the single person, just as human rights and cosmopolitan right do.

Q. *In the course of half a century along the unitary path, Europe has sought to become a model for the "new citizenship." Theorists and jurists have gone so far as to speak of a new paradigm of political liberty capable of separating citizenship from national belonging: a revolution no less radical than that of 1789. But do you not reckon that, put to the test by the flow of migrants, the European myth is at risk of becoming blurred?*

A. Faced with the disembarking of refugees from the poorest areas of the world and with the knotty problem of the political status of the migrants, nation-states are once again the protagonists, and their borders are in the process of becoming more impermeable, with an increased bureaucracy over documents and repatriation. The Europe of cooperation between peoples no longer seems so sure about wishing to be the laboratory of a "new democratic citizenship." And perhaps the decision of the Court of Justice of the European Union a few years ago to reject the Italian ruling of 2011—which instituted the crime of clandestinity—is to be read as an invitation from the Europe of rights to the Europe of politics to temper its inclination to identify itself with the nation and its borders. But, irrespective of what Europe wants or does not want, the migrants are now a part of its identity: of what it is and of what it will be. They are the litmus test of the European myth and of democratic civilization.

The so-called stateless migrants are a global phenomenon: persons who for the most diverse reasons are not able to prove that they have a nationality, either because the state from which they come has ceased to exist, on account of civil wars, or because those fleeing have to keep their identities secret in order to avoid repression by their own state. For many desperate persons, not having identity papers is a strategy they employ to defend their very lives; the problem is that as "human beings" and nothing else, they risk becoming universally vulnerable. In the twentieth century, ethnic cleansing was practiced, turning Jews and members of some European ethnic minorities into noncitizens and so making it possible to deport and eliminate them en masse. In 1954 the United Nations adopted the Convention Relating to the Status of Stateless Persons, with the aim of rendering it impossible for anyone not to have a state. In 1961 many countries signed the convention, pledging to guarantee nationality to stateless people born on their territory. Yet this commitment is not always honored, and very frequently stateless persons are at the mercy of the current potentate.

Democratic cosmopolitanism ought to take it upon itself to engage on this front, in order to devise new institutions and new norms that protect whoever is not part of a state but only a member of humanity, if one can put it like that. This population of the stateless represents a call for a new political identity, one born in the interstices of state jurisdictions or between the oppressive law of their states of origin and the equally oppressive law (at any rate toward them) of the states on whose shores they land. In the former case they are oppressed as subjects of a state, in the latter as nonsubjects of the state to which they report as migrants.

It is in such an identity, outside of state law, that a new citizenship is crystallizing not as an institutionalized belonging but as an act of self-determination reclaiming a voice and thus recognition. It is a nascent democratic citizenship, as it radically denounces a condition of utter subjection, claiming not just human but civil and political rights, as Andreas Kalyvas has observed.

Q. There do exist international conventions on migrants that safe-guard their fundamental human rights, beginning with humanitarian relief and with medical aid.

A. Migrants enjoy, thanks to international conventions, fundamental human rights: the right to humanitarian and medical aid, the right to bare survival. But, as Hannah Arendt wrote, migrants are not granted a legal and political space; they are not granted the right to organize in public as autonomous beings but only to survive as in nature, outside the family of nations and states. The paradox of human rights is that in order for them to be respected, their subjects must be stripped of their political voice and become objects of repression. Because they lack documents, migrants are legally nonexistent, forced to become politically active outside the law. By infringing the law and crossing borders, they earn their entry into the system of law and acquire civil rights to a defense counsel in court or to treatment without violence and torture.

On the occasion of the revolt in Greece, in December 2008, migrants have shown a new willingness to use political language, to exercise some form of citizenship. It happened again in Rosarno, in southern Italy, at the beginning of 2010, when African seasonal workers organized themselves in order to fight back against their condition of semislavery. It happened again in a detention camp in Australia, where more than three hundred migrants decided to hold a hunger strike in order to gain an audience with Australian government officials and voice their request not to be repatriated to Afghanistan, from which they had fled. They selected representatives among themselves and asked for interlocutors with bargaining authority, just as we citizens do when we seek to have our voice heard. To citizens of a democratic state that voice is given by the constitution; to stateless migrants it is denied in spite of the human rights they enjoy.

The clear self-proclamation of political subjectivity is an important step for migrants because it admits that human rights alone do not give them the power to resist repatriation or to claim lawful treatment in the reception centers to which they are confined as soon as they reach the shores of an European state. But what citizenship is possible outside the space of the state? The juridical order, including Europe, does not contemplate a political identity outside state jurisdiction. But migrants who request political rights as human beings look to a supranational and cosmopolitan citizenship.

Q. But what kind of citizenship is possible outside the space of the state?

A. The juridical order in which domestic and international politics are given their structure is founded upon the state and cannot countenance a political identity outside of the state: not even a European one, which does however aspire to be supranational. Yet these migrants lay claim to the dignity of political speech and advance a demand for representation in the name of themselves as human beings: they cry out for what until today has been a utopia, in other words, a cosmopolitan form of political right. They assert that human rights without a political voice do not safeguard them against arbitrariness and oppression, even if they do protect them from death. They maintain that having a voice, being the authors of negotiations and challenges, being political persons, is a right on a par with human right. They say, in short, that the right to citizenship is a fundamental human right before being a legal status.

This is the important novelty that emerges from the recent movements of stateless migrants. Theirs is an important challenge to the progressive and democratic forces of Europe: since it must undoubtedly be possible to reconcile the wholly reasonable calls to regulate migratory flows with a continent-wide project that allows the dignity of citizenship to the migrants, a "voice" or recognized capacity to propose and to discuss, to negotiate and to have some form of representation, even if they do not belong to the body politic of the state that they hail as temporary guests. Setting out from an unprejudiced reading of these experiences is the minimal condition for devising juridical and political solutions that may afford the migrants dignity and that, at the same time, may promote the idea of a European political community that is not only myth or propaganda.

To go back to the discourse regarding cosmopolitanism and to grasp its essential characteristics, we need to pay attention to the way in which the relationship between civil society and politics is understood. In one vision of contemporary cosmopolitanism that I would call "poststate," the natural site of democracy is held to be in civil society, the sphere in which persons can attain the self-management of their voluntary relationships. In the other vision, which I would call "postnation," the natural site of democracy is the political sphere, and the goal is the constitutionalization of the relationships between states. The first approach is wedded either to a liberal free-market vision or to a libertarian and anticoercive vision: it interprets democracy more as a civic culture of associationism, of participation, and of mobilization than as a political process of decision making that occurs within a state. This is the position of, for example, Richard Falk, the former professor of international law at Princeton, the author in the past of a memorable public intervention against the Vietnam War.

Devoted to cosmopolitanism, Falk's last writings express a profound dissatisfaction with the form of the state within which democracy has been forced to live. His theoretical and ideal hinterland is libertarian, in that he emphasizes the aspect of democratic action that exalts grassroots movements far more than it does decision-making procedures. In this vision, civil society is the most authentic site of participation and of liberty because it is antagonistic toward the organized power of the state. Agonistic democracy and the libertarian myth of a self-governing society encounter each other in this radical vision of cosmopolitanism. In this reading, cosmopolitan democracy is identified with a postmodern vision of democracy and a poststate perspective on politics: democracy without state sovereignty and in the guise of a politics of the movements.

Q. However, the political approach to democratic cosmopolitanism is more alert to the relationship between civil society and the political sphere.

A. It considers civil society to be the abode of a liberty that, if not regulated by politics, may herald domination. It recognizes the social movements and the NGOs as components of global democracy and the site of a more authentic representation than an electoral representation, but at the same time it holds that, in the absence of institutionalized procedures of decision making and supervision, the social movements and the NGOs can be or become a factor of unsupervised power that rewards the agency of the new elites. If we scrutinize these new, informal venues of participation we cannot gainsay the fact that they mobilize only a few citizens while making the many (in the name of whom the self-selected few speak) even more passive. As Jane Mansbridge has observed, since participants volunteer, those who have the most intense interest in participation or a louder voice will often dominate. Daniele Archibugi's writings approach cosmopolitan democracy from the angle of international political bodies vested with the power to approve and validate decisions taken in response to the globalization of civil society and to violations of human rights. Cosmopolitanism is based here on the following argument: since civil society lacks universality of citizenship (the common good), it is exposed to the power of the strongest and can give rise to a sort of new state of nature. This vision of cosmopolitan democracy is not without contradictions. The challenges it has to face are twofold: that of territorial political power and that of globally diffused economic power, of states and of financial capitalism. To tell the truth, the defenders of democratic cosmopolitanism have manifested a measure of myopia toward states. On the one hand, they have maintained that states are powerful enough to harm their own citizens; on the other hand, they have acknowledged that they are not powerful enough to protect their citizens from the harm inflicted by new global actors. States, they seem to be saying, are powerful against single individuals but powerless against vested interests.

While the globalization of the economy does not erode the coercive power of the state, it does attenuate its capacity to pursue policies of social justice. Is this the paradox of our times? The extraordinary escalation of economic and financial globalization renders states less sovereign in their decision-making power but also less democratic insofar as they forbear to exercise their sovereignty of decision over welfare spending and market regulation. However, this critical conjuncture does not render states either obsolete or weaker. This paradox of weakness in programming politics and strength in exercising their coercive power over ordinary citizens has led some scholars to anticipate and hope for something more than an "interstate" democracy. For example, Thomas Pogge and Charles Beitz have argued for an international coordination vested with sufficient power "to interfere in the internal affairs" of states, indeed, to weaken them when issues of social justice are at stake.

But while there is no certainty that the neo-Kantian strategy of constitutionalizing states would actually change the international relations between them, so as to make them also based on explicit and voluntary consent, as we have mentioned above, it would also not be able to alter the logic itself of the international order because it would not place national sovereignty in doubt. The expansion of the geosocial space produced by globalization calls into question the construction of a new geopolitical space, but there is no certainty as to the practicability and the forms of this evolution in a juridical sense. On the other hand, the state space within which democracy has been put into practice no longer seems sufficient to guarantee its functioning. And in order to protect democracy within states it would seem to be necessary to construct a global political order capable of regulating finance and of imposing norms on the civil society that has ramified beyond the borders of states. In short, as Jean L. Cohen has argued in her recent work, it seems as if politics ought to do at a global level what in the course of the last two centuries it has done at a national level, namely, initiate a constitutionalization of power relations. The European experiment is an important model in this regard.

Where I differ from the advocates of cosmopolitan democracy is in my reluctance to accept their critique of the state form. Nonetheless, the project of politicizing classical cosmopolitanism is an important one, not least because it serves to open up new and useful lines of theoretico-political enquiry into constitutionalizing international relations.

Q. Can you be more specific in your critique of democratic cosmopolitanism?

A. I think that the "postnation" dimension should prove of greater interest to us than the "poststate" one because the nub of the problem for democratic cosmopolitanism is the nation-state rather than the state as a legal and political form of collective life under the rule of law. States, Archibugi has argued, are "the greatest holders of power on earth," responsible for an enforced cultural homogenization at the national level ("Principles of Cosmopolitan Democracy," in *Reimagining Political Community* [Cambridge: Polity, 1998]). "It is states that have armed forces; control police; mint currency; permit or refuse entrance to their lands; states that recognize citizens' rights and impose their duties." However, it is unclear why these state prerogatives are a negative fact, above all if one thinks that the alternative could be private corporations or churches minting currency and refusing entrance to their territories. The emancipation of the legal and political power of the state from patrimonialism and theocracy should be carefully disassociated from the long history of the arbitrary use of force and the law that have been perpetrated by state rulers throughout the centuries. In this regard, bureaucratic emancipation from feudal rule and subsequent democratic constitutionalism represented a genuine revolution in the structure and form of the state (and a positive one), not merely an "evolution." Moreover, the welfare-state transformation of the democratic states has not merely been an additional "instrument" the states used to mitigate what they are, that is to say, a "tool of domination." As a matter of fact, the history of the welfare state suggests it is the link between democracy and "national interests" that may vitiate democracy.

Q. *But the international order is not an empty space outside of states and in which states shift around and clash like atoms in space but rather an organized system of norms and conventions that includes all the states and outside of which it is hard to think the states at all.*

A. The great constitutionalist and philosopher of law Hans Kelsen maintained that "the legal order of each State, each national legal order, is organically connected with the international legal order and through this order with every national legal order, so that all legal orders merge into an integrated legal system." According to this interactive conception of sovereignty, every state exists within a delimiting normative order. State sovereignty implies the presence of other sovereignties, and, like individual autonomy, it is always limited. This is the actual condition of its existence. I would like to add, returning to the conversation we were having about historical roots, that democratic cosmopolitanism is an offshoot of a universalism of rights resting upon two pillars: the individual and the nation. From the days of the Abbé de Saint-Pierre, of Kant, and then of the Saint-Simonians, European thinkers and political leaders have seen the association of autonomous nations as a federative pact of mutual aid and of cooperation. The jurists of the twentieth century, not least Kelsen, maintained that the consolidating of the state based upon rights and upon constitutional democracy was a necessary intermediate step toward a global order founded upon law and right. In this tradition, the old continent has found the resources to react to the shame of totalitarianism and of Nazism. The ratification of the Universal Declaration of Human Rights of 1948 and the Treaty of Rome of 1957 have been very important achievements matured in the moral culture of universalism and in the political culture of cosmopolitanism. But we must not forget that the history of our continent also demonstrates that the nation can speak—as all too often it has done—the language of aggressive nationalism or, as today, of ethnic and chauvinist regionalism.

The nation can be interpreted as a claim about the primacy of the interests of one's own group against that of other peoples and other nations. Protectionism, racist policies, xenophobia, and the ideology of national "exceptionalism" have been, and remain still, examples of anticosmopolitan interpretations. This is why the nation more than the state can become an obstacle to universalism, distorting democracy.

Consider, for example, fascism and its conception of nationalism . . .

Q. . . . Are you referring to the period when Italian fascism began to build its own cultural hegemony, depicting itself as heir to the Risorgimento?

A. Giovanni Gentile fabricated an image of Mazzini as harbinger and promoter of the expansionist vocation of the nation, of a nationalistic alternative to the humanitarian and democratic ideologies: ideologies that, in a derogatory sense, Gentile associated with pacifism and solidarity. And he concluded that there are no rights of peoples that other peoples should recognize: because—he explained—"right is conquest" and power, not a curb upon power; it is an expression of might, not a containment of might. For Gentile, then, the right of the nation was "worthy and sacred" and above all opposed to association between nations. The fascist nation smuggled in an imperial project when coopting Mazzini and distorted his ideas of "mission" and duty, using them as justification for enrolling in the fascist militias and for individual sacrifice to the fascist state. But in order to exalt the ends of the authoritarian ethical state, Gentile had to strip Mazzini's nation of its international cooperative mission and to excise its universalistic ideal. In this exaltation of duty to the nation and of the overcoming of individual egoisms by nationalist and fascist philosophy were prefigured a particularistic ideology and the primacy of the vitalistic specificity of one nation over and against the others. The abandonment of universalism in the name of the priority of the nation is capable of twisting democracy itself toward nationalist solutions and does not have fascist inflections only: it can manifest itself in the guise of ethnocentric or communitarian democracies such as some parties and countries seem to be intent upon resurrecting in Europe. Defeated as a totalitarian state, fascism is still alive as an ideology.

Q. You maintain that while the most representative philosophical culture is marked by universalism, though one attuned to what is specific and particular, the political dimension seems to follow an opposite trajectory. Why do you distinguish between the political and the philosophical level?

A. It is undoubtedly the case that in the universities and in symposia the universalistic philosophies are hegemonic today. Political liberalism and the theory of rights are not easily contested and rejected. There have certainly been adaptations, revisions, critiques, and also attempts to harmonize local and universal knowledge, multiculturalism and liberalism. For example, after more than twenty years of debate the communitarians have tempered their particularistic positions, and philosophical currents of an individualist character have sought to situate the idea of personal flourishing in the social and cultural context, so as to render justice more sensitive to the well-being of the concrete person rather than to that of an abstract individual. This tendency is exemplified by the writings of Martha Nussbaum and Amartya Sen. But this theoretical framework structured in universalistic terms is restricted to the academic milieu. Outside of which, in the everyday reality in which we live, and in particular in the European West, the scenario is different and never readily welcomes those who are different, even when these latter strive to integrate.

I will give myself leave to retell a story I read on the blog www .stranieriinitalia.it, where Amilca Ismael, an Italian citizen who came originally from Mozambique and has been working for years in a care home for the elderly, recounts her experience as an immigrant.

When you leave your country of origin and live for so many years in another country, a strange mechanism is released within you because, in order to insert yourself in your new life, you need to set aside your habits. And this completely changes your way of thinking and of seeing things, but your roots do nonetheless remain, and this causes you a great deal of confusion. . . . Another sad thing is that, despite having an Italian passport, despite working like any other Italian and paying taxes, in short despite my also making a contribution to the country, I bear always and anyway the stigma of "undocumented" alien that accompanies me in my daily round, that marginalizes me on account ✓of my roots and does not allow people to see me for what I truly am.

Q. In the personal experience of Amilca Ismael two levels of discourse seem to intersect, one of a moral-existential character and the other of a normative-political character.

A. On the one hand, we recognize a person's relationship with their own roots as an indispensable precondition for cultivating her memory in a present that is generative of new and different memories (hence the unhealable breach in an emigrant's life between her identity before and afterward, with the resulting sense of never feeling at home in her own world). On the other hand, we recognize the relationship in the adopted country between the wider culture (often a wider prejudice) and the laws: a relationship that is contradictory and complex, although this complexity is particularly prone to coming to light when the wider culture measures itself against non-European and non-Western cultures.

Q. Amilca Ismael's story can be used as an example of the launching of the multicultural process in European—and, in this case, Italian— civilization.

A. The philosophers of politics have generally focused upon the normative-political aspect, their intention being to weigh up the relationship between universalism of liberal rights and pluralism, that is, between a conception of liberty that rests upon the priority of the individual (liberty as noninterference) and a conception that instead claims the cultural dimension as its precondition, in order that liberty protected by rights be effectively enjoyed. Yet, just when theoretical reflection seems to have metabolized multiculturalism and, with convincing justifications, to have married difference and minority rights—accepting, for example, the idea of social rights and, in part also, cultural rights—European civil society discovers the existence of the "problem" of difference. What for political philosophy is a justified and accepted fact is for the general public and opinion at large a risk to be neutralized and even a violation of the good of national identity. The paradox of our times is the fact that in our conferences we discuss multiculturalism, appealing then to reasonableness, while news reports daily present a snapshot of a public opinion that is often intolerant and insensitive to reasons of right when they are used to justify cultural diversity and religious pluralism or that is reluctant to accept difference instead of merely enduring it. The diachronic relationship between intellectual reflection and public opinion often goes unnoticed in the specialist literature. Yet it is a fact that while we write about the idea of equal rights as if it were a shared value, it is in fact very far from being a shared common sense.

Q. Yet the Declaration of Human Rights by the United Nations, signed in Paris in December 1948, spoke out loud and clear: "All human beings are born free and equal in dignity. They are endowed with reason and conscience, and should act towards one another in the spirit of fraternity."

A. Peoples arrived at the Declaration of Human Rights after immense cruelties and suffering. At the origin of what we are today, there is the Holocaust itself and with it the extermination of millions of Gypsies and antifascists, the suppression of the different. It was necessary for the survivors of the war and of those violences to promise in turn, in the name of a human condition common to one and all, to do what up until then no one had succeeded in doing, namely, as far as possible to prevent politics and right being disassociated. Nor should this commitment be limited to some states only, that is to say, to those who had won on the field of battle. Every people and every state had to subscribe to the pact on behalf of humanity. To achieve this, it was necessary to transcend and oppose a communitarian conception of equality, that is to say, a conception whereby the free are deemed to be free because equal in some specific respect that cannot be extended to others. Particular factors like race or nation should no longer be used as a condition for attributing to or depriving persons of rights of liberty. The Declaration of Paris and the democratic constitutions arose in opposition to the Nazi and Fascist totalitarian experiments and as radical responses to ethnocentric or identitary visions of political belonging. In the aftermath of World War II there was therefore a turning point, and a promise was made—though unfortunately one that has been too often brushed aside, as in the France of Nicholas Sarkozy, which in 2010 expelled thousands of Roma with one-way tickets. The fact that it has been set aside does not alter the just reason behind that promise, which, like a Kantian "as if," is a regulative idea that, if it does not promise an end to the violations, at least sustains the existence of laws, conventions, and moral values that enable us to denounce those violations. The idea that underpins this promise is that henceforth no one will go unpunished for atrocities and war crimes. No invader and no tyrant will manage to find a hiding place on earth. The true success of the regulative idea of respect for human rights lies in this: in having defeated the idea that wars and crimes are justified, perhaps in the name of reason of state.

Q. *The decision of the Elysées Palace to expel the Roma gave rise to furious polemics in France and throughout Europe. What in your opinion was the gravest aspect of this affair?*

A. The fact that the Roma were repatriated as a group. Many political forces in France, just as in Italy, proclaimed a crisis in the universalism of rights and bore responsibility for an arrogant return to policies that close borders and plan and carry out mass expulsions. Article 19 of the Charter of Rights of the European Union establishes that "Collective expulsions are forbidden." In the text, there is the echo of European twentieth-century history: those terrible tragedies that were consummated in the elimination of individuals whose "fault" was to belong to the "wrong" race or to a national or religious minority. The roots of the European Union are in the extermination camps: this memory must be our point of departure when we judge the actions of democratically elected governments.

We have consoled ourselves by saying that the Gypsies expelled from France were not, when all is said and done, dispatched to concentration camps; that they had been "invited" to go away and were then accompanied to the frontier with a ticket in their pockets paid for by the taxpayer. But the "polite" form of accompanying persons to the border, with their tickets already purchased, does not alter the very grave nature of the deed we have witnessed without, unfortunately, our having been sufficiently troubled by it: a collective discrimination, a violation of the liberty of persons—as it happens, European persons—because of what they are and of their identity, a clear breach of Article 21 of the Charter of the Union. For this article does indeed state that "any discrimination based on any ground such as sex, race, colour, ethnic or social origin, genetic features, language, religion or belief, political or any other opinion, membership of a national minority, property, birth, disability, age or sexual orientation shall be prohibited."

Q. Yet universalism is making noteworthy strides in the juridical sphere: for example, in the laws on pedophilia that have internationalized such crimes, rendering them liable to prosecution even in countries other than those in which they were committed.

A. It is quite true that in civil society, in law, and in the economy notable progress has been and is being recorded. But universalism does not appear to be gaining ground in the political sphere, which consists of powers, parties, and institutions, in systems for the creation of public opinion, and, finally, in the ethical culture of the society at large. Today's challenge may be rendered therefore as follows: how can we manage things so that politics and public opinion are able to keep pace with globalization without betraying the idea of equal respect due to all human beings?

As we saw when speaking of the need for a cosmopolitan level of quasi citizenship for whoever is outside of their own state (and is thereby exposed to the might of the "host" states), the challenge to the democratic ethos of inclusion and equal respect comes precisely from the grounding of democratic legitimacy (equality in political inclusion) within national identity. One could conclude that such a merging of democracy with the nation is inevitable and that democracy has perforce to come to terms with the identitary nature of politics: certainly with one identity in particular, that of the nation. It is not a question of denying our diverse identities as people speaking different languages and relying upon different historical memories but of understanding that, alongside or above this level of belonging, it is important we identify a level that is political in an independent way from the national.

In this regard, there is an institutional lacuna. And we are also discovering just how difficult it is to strengthen the European Parliament and to impart a political direction to the European Union, in order that this latter not remain confined or subjected to the national states but acquires an autonomy of decision that has the power to withstand and defeat nationalist resistances to a common European polity.

Q. You alluded earlier to the risks run by the process of European integration: which of them strike you as the most serious?

A. Until recently, the weakness of democratic legitimacy was rooted in EU institutions, not the European project itself, which, in terms of its self-representation to its citizens and to the world, has embodied widely shared "universal values" and presented itself as a beacon of "the inviolable and inalienable rights of the human person, freedom, democracy, equality and the rule of law," as stated in the preamble to the Lisbon Treaty. Democratic cosmopolitanism, which is a key chapter in contemporary democratic theory, is a creation of a pro-Europe, utopian approach intended to extend democratic principles beyond national borders, in order to govern economic globalization and protect democracy. In relation to these principles, the "democratic deficit" has been blamed for the incomplete political integration of the European Union: while bureaucratic competencies have grown stronger, political bodies have, in terms of accountability, yet to develop beyond the chrysalis stage. This narrative has recently changed. Many Europeans now question the validity and even legitimacy of the European Union as a political project.

One certain consequence of the interruption of the political integration process has been the burgeoning of an "executive dominance" (such that the European Union seems to belong to the same category as "enlightened despotism") that, together with the economic crisis, has turned out to be one of the factors to have triggered populist euroskepticism. A remote European leadership that operates beyond the reach of any democratic controls has only served to exacerbate the power imbalance between member states: this, among other accusations being leveled at the European Union, is what threatens to undermine consensus on the ideals behind the European Union. Executive dominance and euroskeptic ideology exist in an osmotic relationship. The consequence is that today, in public opinion, a declaration of loyalty to principles risks seeming like an ideological construct designed to serve a status quo where, in fact, the political behavior of the European leadership follows a logic of its own, one impervious to the economic problems that many Europeans are facing. At the level of the member states there is evident a frontal attack, systematic and tenacious, on inclusion and individual rights, especially pertaining to those who are weakest and therefore most in need of rights.

In the everyday life of many European societies we are witnessing the rebirth of ethnic communitarianism, an ideological platform that relaunches the idea of the purity of purportedly atavistic traditions. In the national elections held in Hungary in 2010 and in the Low Countries in 2012 (just to mention some cases) we have seen the growth of nationalist and even fascist parties, and this takes us far from the promise made by the European peoples at the end of World War II.

Q. *Do you fear that our constitutions do not shield us sufficiently from fascist forms of anti-individualist reaction?*

A. This concern is wholly justified because we have never sought to cure the profound evil at the origin of such phenomena, namely, the nationalistic foundations of the European democracies, which sprang from an identitary factor that has never been dissolved or, if one can put it like this, amended. It is true that the nations have in the long run had a democratic and emancipatory function. It is true that in the second half of the twentieth century they have been turned into "nations of citizens and not of members," as Jürgen Habermas put it. But now, perhaps also because of declining prosperity, we are witnessing a rebirth of the nations in a nonpolitical guise and the recrudescence of prejudice in the strong ethnic nations (those of northern Europe) toward the "uncivic" nations (those of southern Europe). There is thus a risk of rights becoming associated with an ethnic inheritance, in the sense of being identified with ownership of the soil, culture, language, religion, ethnicity, and even of "civism" itself.

Q. *What consequences does the degeneration of the concept of ownership have for the field of rights?*

A. The idea of we ourselves being the legitimate owners of what we call "our" land, or "our" nation, or indeed "our" constitution leads us to interpret rights as instrumental to a goal that lies beyond them, as a good that claims fulfillment at any cost; rights do not temper the possessive vision in this case but overwhelm it. Thus, when people say that they "want to keep immigrants out," we are being referred not so much or not only to a physical action of protecting borders as to a symbolic and cultural exclusion from citizenship of those immigrants who live in our country, work, respect the laws, and pay taxes. To the objection "why this exclusion?" we hear the answer: "The rights belong to us."

Q. What is the reason, in your opinion, for the failure to adjust the constitution? And why has universalism become something so cold, so bureaucratic, and so normative?

A. When, between 1946 and 1948, the constitutions of the countries having emerged from totalitarianism, such as Italy and Germany, were drafted, and the French constitution was likewise rewritten, theorists of democracy from Raymond Aron to Norberto Bobbio had rightly warned of the risk of essentializing political values. They were reflecting critically on the experience of "hyperessentialization" and on the myth of the ethical state—capable, in conjunction, of transforming the state into a totalitarian project. For Aron's and Bobbio's generation, norms, rules, and the impartiality of legal process were the site of liberty; they paid less attention to the formative—or, if you will, the metaprocedural—dimension of democracy.

Q. Does democracy perhaps have an ethos?

A. Aron and Bobbio, though having different approaches to liberalism and the struggle for liberty, believed that institutions and procedures could manage the work of politics on their own. For them and above all from the Cold War onward, democracy was first and foremost a technics of decision making and an institutional system, the opposite of a regime that, as in the Soviet model, identified democracy with the instantiation of substantive equality. That is to say, its principal value lay in its being a method for deliberation and conflict resolution within a condition of free and open competition between a plurality of political options and in view of achieving a majority. If anything, it was liberalism that would be the repository of values, primarily that of individual liberty. Democracy did not have an essential value, save inasmuch as it rendered possible the peaceful resolution of disagreement and conflict. It was because of its capacity to replace violence that democracy was worthy of being called such, even if it did not fulfill any other values (like rationality or preference representation) or engender any other outcomes (like economic equality or redistribution). Making political decisions through elections was valuable in itself, especially in societies with insurmountable conflicts of value and interests. Elections avoided violence by enabling opposing groups to alternate in power while giving losers incentives to wait until the next election instead of opposing the winner through violence—which happens if winning is truly possible in the next round and if the payoffs for winning in future rounds are greater than those of immediate violence. Clearly, alternation can induce moderation in office when rebellion is sufficiently costly, such that even a ruler who could manipulate rules in his own interest would not do so in order to avoid violence. This containing aspect rendered democracy valuable.

Winston Churchill's quip of 1947—"Democracy is the worst form of government, except for all those other forms of government that have been tried from time to time"—has become in postwar Western Europe a universal maxim. In sum, we cannot do without democracy, even if democracy is not the best possible form of government because it allows "numbers" or "quantity" to rule, rather than competences.

Democratic thought so conceived had some evident limitations, which perhaps Habermas alone has sought to repair, placing his trust in rational dialogue within society and among citizens, as individuals and groups, and not only in the "rules of the game" and the political contest. Habermas acknowledged the importance of procedures but considered them insufficient on their own for a normative justification of democracy. A similar view was shared by John Rawls, who also recognized that political groups are inevitable in the electoral arena; however, he believed that a democracy that merely consists in a bargain between groups is unsuited to a just society because it induces citizens to "take a narrow or group-interest standpoint" instead of aiming at a conception of the common good.

Habermas's critique was more far reaching. It identified proceduralism with Schumpeterian realism and a method that was morally agnostic. For Habermas, although "public controversies among several parties" are a necessary condition for democratic decision making, they do not guarantee reasonable outcomes. Therefore, Habermas proposed to identify the conditions under which autonomous deliberation could be achieved through democratic procedures, such that the latter could pave the way to a "rationally motivated consensus." This is the most specific trait of Habermas's theory of deliberative democracy, which, although it defends democracy in procedural terms, stresses the substantive goals that procedures should attain and focuses on the (ideal) conditions under which they could be achieved (for instance, autonomy, reciprocity, and sincerity, conditions without which deliberation would be nothing else but the struggle for power employing electoral means). Nevertheless, the normative goal of deliberative democracy is not so different from that goal advocated by procedural democracy. For Habermas, the main goal of the democratic process is autonomous decision making—that is, the public discussion of decisions with freedom from coercion and from socioeconomic subordination. The idea that democracy can produce good-quality outcomes and approach consensus is subordinate to and derived from autonomy, since the latter will enable reason-based, and hence tendentially consensual, decisions. On this procedural idea, Bobbio would also agree. Yet the main difference between these two theorists consisted in the fact that Habermas focused his political theory on an "ideal speech situation" where autonomy can be said to exist and consensus likely to happen, and he took that situation to be a regulative ideal that real political processes should "mirror"; procedural democrats like Bobbio, instead, believe that equal freedom can be striven for in nonideal scenarios, even if deliberation does not take place and if consent is not attained, because bargaining and voting are also legitimate mechanisms for expressing the majority view, especially in contexts of profound disagreement. The aspect that Habermas and Bobbio (along with other like-minded proceduralists) share is that both proposed to free politics from ethical encumbrances so as to anchor it in procedures and in the forging of social relationships founded upon reasoned opinions, not because the actors have been educated in civic virtues by the state or compulsory participation but because, interacting in accordance with rights and the guidelines for deliberation, they learn to respect one another and to resolve disagreements through the force of sound arguments. Yet whereas Bobbio accepted the "rules of the game" as indicative of a political community prepared to resolve its disagreements yet not overcome them, Habermas's theory of deliberation invites us to consider the counting of votes and majority rule as an admission that interests and predetermined opinions still guide public behavior. Habermas's conception of democracy is meant to overcome or amend a purely instrumental and functional approach to decision making and procedures. Bobbio was never convinced that this would be necessary or even desirable. What distinguishes these two authors is perhaps the attitude to pluralism and conflict: in a word, Bobbio has a more benign relationship to liberalism.

Q. Let us go back to Bobbio, who arguably was the most important intellectual and the one who best represents the history of Italian postwar democratization.

A. Bobbio's articles between the end of the war and the drafting of the Italian constitution, that is, between 1945 and 1947, were written in the style of an intellectual Enlightenment that addressed reason rather than the passions and that abhorred rhetoric and ideological polemic. His style was thus in keeping with the proper mode of operation of democratic institutions: "educating citizens to freedom" in the conviction that, if placed in circumstances such that liberty could be used as the norms and rules indicate, they would understand its value and defend it reasonably and with tenacity. Democratic custom, Bobbio seemed to be saying in these pioneering writings, does not take shape outside of and in the absence of democratic institutions. In this "institutionalist" vision his interlocutors were those intellectuals who had fought in the Resistance and were involved in various guises in the politics of constitutionalization: activists, members of the Italian Constituent Assembly (elected on June 2, 1946), teachers, civil servants, magistrates, and, in general, educated citizens.

Q. Up until 1947, the object of Bobbio's struggle was the democratization of the state and, more precisely, the institutionalization of authority and the impartiality of the law.

A. And his main concern was the demolition of the structure and of the ideology of the ethical state inherited from fascism. Consequently, he held that the most urgent task of the members of the Constituent Assembly (which met from June 1946 to the end of 1947) was to establish a legal framework that would guarantee the state's independence from all ideologies, religious or secular, championed by the church or by the parties.

To understand Bobbio's position, we should remember that early in the twentieth century (he was born in 1909) democratic procedures had been fiercely challenged from the Left and the Right—the former criticized democracy's incapacity to deliver redistribution, the latter its failure to maintain stability. Against those challenges and the defenses of autocratic regimes they often entailed, theorists such as Kelsen and Bobbio defended procedural democracy from a normative perspective, arguing that it was the best (or perhaps the only adequate) way of protecting the political freedom of all members of society. In particular, Bobbio viewed the failure of the Weimar Republic in 1933 as emblematic of all that the Italian constitution should avoid, the latter's success ultimately depending on its capacity to radically democratize the structure of the state and to regulate party pluralism. Choices such as universal suffrage and electoral representation, in fact the democratic transformation of the legislative body, were necessary but not sufficient. Democracy required a normative change in the legal and institutional framework of the state and of the ethico-juridical culture of its functionaries and then a general reinterpretation of political categories.

Read sixty years later, the political articles written by Bobbio in the period 1945–1947 seem to be lessons in democratic theory centered around the Weberian distinction between the two forms of politics: politics as the functioning of institutions, with impartiality of the law and civil servants as the fundamental precondition of citizenship, and politics as the terrain of political confrontation between different and conflicting proposals advanced with a view to defining a majority. Thus, Bobbio had in his sights the two opposed approaches to the defascistification of the state that emerged in those years: the myth of the "apoliticality" of political techniques and the opposite myth of "pan-politics." His Enlightenment cast of mind was sustained by the conviction that it was necessary to exclude faithlike ideologies from the institutional domain. But, according to Bobbio, the regular use of democratic procedures was eminently political and civic because it would enable citizens to understand that liberty is a value, not simply a mechanical exercise, and is the precondition of an ethic of political responsibility.

One could say that in the years of the Constituent Assembly Bobbio sought to inspire a sort of *Verfassungspatriotismus*, the "constitutional patriotism" of which Habermas spoke later on, although Bobbio himself never admitted as much, perhaps because in Italy fascism had for decades an unquestioned monopoly over the use and meaning of the term "patriotism" and moreover because he was no doubt impatient with communitarian values such as the fatherland. Nonetheless, being a democrat, he felt it to be his responsibility to play his part in the formation of a civic Italy or, as he wrote, paraphrasing Gramsci, to make a revolution without revolutionary instruments.

Q. *The Cold War radically changed things.*

A. Yes, fostering a dogmatic approach to politics, and considering faithlike ideologies to be deaf to dialogue, it meant to Bobbio that citizens would be unable to accept the deliberative and open-minded potentials of democracy, which would then be simply a method for obtaining a majority. From spring 1947 onward, when Alcide De Gasperi returned from the United States waving the check the Allies had given him in exchange for his break with the government of national unity (a coalition government comprising Christian Democrats, Communists, and Socialists), political confrontation took on the character of *odium theologicum*. In that climate, Bobbio recalibrated his intellectual interventions, employing a more procedural and normative, less ethico-pedagogic style, one more anchored to a minimalist vision—as we would put it today—of democracy. Bobbio's dislike of "political sectarianism" and of the spirit of "holy war" reinforced his inclination toward a realistic vision of politics and his conviction that a secularized politics (that is, a politics without dogmatic ideologies) would involve shifting the conflict from a plane of absolute opposition (and a true/false antagonism) to one of competition between political programs. Without this shift, there would not have been room for deliberation because, he wrote, "if the political struggle is phrased, not in terms of social or economic, that is to say, utilitarian debate but in terms of theological, philosophical, or moralistic dispute, agreement is not even thinkable." Far from being an expression of toleration toward the communists, Bobbio's politics of dialogue, in which he engaged in 1954 with Palmiro Togliatti, the general secretary of the PCI, was wholly consistent with a deliberative vision of democratic politics and with the defense of an open society. Bobbio challenged the communists on three related topics: the theory of the state, the philosophical character of Marxism, and the theory of liberty. To keep the door open to the "illiberals" did not imply relativism or the passive acceptance of any opinion—failure to understand this basic fact led later critics to interpret, wrongly, Bobbio's dialogue with the PCI as a sign of weakness rather than strength. The dialogue with the PCI reinforced Bobbio's conviction that it was crucial to link the defense of individual liberty to the defense of democracy and thus to avoid the dualism between negative and positive liberty, liberalism and democracy, a trait common to both Cold War liberals and their adversaries on the Left. Indeed, his *politics of dialogue* with the "enemies" of liberal democracy enabled him to overcome the Manichean logic of the Cold War, since he looked for his interlocutors outside the borders constructed by the politics of the two blocs, and in doing so he defied the anticommunist theorem that was shaping Italian politics and that in fact outlived the Cold War. Bobbio's politics of dialogue was a democratic riposte to Cold War politics (a Habermasian position *ante litteram*) because its object was to vindicate the educative potential of the democratic process and, conversely, the antidemocratic implications of dogmatism.

The fact is that once the Italian communists had agreed to debate with a liberal theorist over their doctrine, and following a Socratic method, they were also agreeing to discuss their ideological system and hence to run the risk of acknowledging its limits. In actual fact, the politics of dialogue would have had a broader impact because, if the communists had accepted Bobbio's challenge to make a revolution without revolutionary instruments, their participation in the dialogue would have reinforced his trust in their loyalty to democracy. Bobbio wrote: "I believe that democracy needs, indeed, has an ever greater need, of intellectuals acting as mediators. Allow me to take it as a good sign that Roderigo di Castiglia [the nom de plume of Palmiro Togliatti] has felt obliged to reply to one of them."

Q. Was it a sign of weakness on Bobbio's part to have decided that one could and should enter into a dialogue with the communists?

A. Quite the reverse. His stance was radically anticommunist precisely because it was antithetical to the spirit of the Cold War, or incompatible with the idea that the limits to participation in political dialogue could be deduced from premises external to the actual reasons for the dialogue. Bobbio's logic was in essence consistent with what we, using a language we have become familiar with only recently, would call the logic of "democratic deliberation." Participating in the political dialogue with the premise that some ideas could not undergo transformations, that is to say, be a genuine object of dialogue, meant an a priori mortgaging of the outcome of the discourse and hence a disparaging of political liberty. The limits on political decision making—the rights and the rules of democratic decision making—are set by the political interlocutors themselves. This is what a democratic constitution means. Conversely, limits imposed for nonpolitical reasons, fideistic or ideological as they may be, are like acts of command and vetoes external to democratic deliberation. Bobbio's aversion to "political sectarianism" and the spirit of "holy war" may explain his inclination toward a realist vision of politics and his conviction that a secularized politics entailed the transformation of conflicts from an absolute enmity into an antagonism between vested interests and political programs. Without this transformation, he wrote, there would be no room for deliberation: "if we believe that political struggle is an antagonism that rests not on a discussion over social and economic issues, but on a theological, moralistic, or philosophical disputation, any agreement would be unthinkable." Bobbio was opposing what today is known as "militant democracy" or the exclusion of adversaries from political competition. I take his teaching to be an invitation to accept a conflictual view of democracy and a refusal to make even constitutional principles a matter of metaphysical notions of human dignity, while insisting that they offer guidance in the practical exercise of democratic capacities and participation. This is a profession of immanentism, which is entirely consistent with democracy. To embrace it wholeheartedly would require endorsing a view of democracy that is radically political and procedural, not identified with any desirable outcome, and nonperfectionist. Democracy as a process of making and revising decisions and opinions based on having an equal share in power: this is an interpretation that accepts the risks arising from liberty, although it does not renounce judging which movements are or are not consistent with civic constitutionalism. The "rules-of-the-game" perspective, which Bobbio had espoused since 1945, includes all as partisans of different (and somewhat divergent) interpretations. It is up to democratic citizens to make sure that the more expansive views win and that the constitution is interpreted in view of enlarging rather than narrowing its principles. Yet there is no guarantee that the good will prevail and no certainty as to the stability and duration of democracy. An inclusive politics, such as democracy offers, entails making the citizens of each generation responsible guardians of their constitution, guardians capable of understanding which domains require maintenance and adjustment and prepared to risk doing so without limiting political liberty and the equal opportunity to participate. We cannot embrace a militant conception of democracy and exclude adversaries *ex ante.*

4

The "Few" and the "Many"

Q. In recent decades the gap between rich and poor has grown steadily throughout the world. According to the data from the OECD, in 2008 the average income of the richest 10 percent of Italians was ten times higher than that of the poorest 10 percent. From 2011 onward Occupy Wall Street and the protests in so many other cities have denounced the growing imbalance between the 1 percent of the wealthiest classes and the remaining 99 percent of the population. What effect is this dynamic likely to have on the health of our democracies?

A. With the eruption of a spontaneous and spectacular movement in the heart of global financial capitalism, one that has deliberately remained leaderless, Occupy Wall Street has highlighted a question that has come to the fore in the last two decades, even if it has really only flared up with the eruption of the economic crisis in 2008. At issue today is the maintenance of the compromise between oligarchy and democracy. Or, to put it another way, what is in doubt is the readiness of the few, or the very few, to remain part of a society that is governed through the votes of everyone and in which, moreover, more and more people are increasingly in need of help because of their impoverishment.

Q. Wait a minute. How do you define oligarchy?

A. I will answer by referring to a book entitled *Oligarchy*, written by Jeffrey Winter. Oligarchy, Winter explains, consists of a concentration of material wealth (concrete possessions) that resists policies of redistribution. It is not simply a group with far-reaching power or an elite, this latter being a term that refers to the selection of a political class, not an oligarchy. It has to do rather with persons who possess extraordinary material wealth and who do not necessarily seek a political role, being able to live under any and every regime. Their primary objective is to protect and increase their wealth. It is not an interest in some future project that spurs them on but the safeguarding (which also means the expansion) of an economic power that they already have. And it is in the light of this power that oligarchies decide whether to abstain from or intervene in the political game. History shows that the advent of a democratic regime has never involved the elimination of the holders of wealth, nor even the expropriation of excessive fortunes. It has, however, involved their being deprived of the privilege of selecting those who make decisions or making political decisions directly. Democracy distributes this power among the large majority of the population by means of universal suffrage. On the other hand, democracy does not presuppose or seek economic equality, nor an equal distribution of property, nor the abolition of private property. Democracy is a political system, not an economic one; it is a system that consists precisely of distributing among all adult citizens the fundamental right to participate in power and to make decisions in a direct or indirect fashion. And it can do this because it blocks the transfer of political power from the socioeconomic to the political dimension, placing something akin to a protective curtain around the institutions and the procedures of decision making so that they may be used by everyone under the same conditions, without distinctions of class, culture, or gender. This is the artificial and general character of political equality that citizenship represents. The development of the democracies has therefore not eliminated the oligarchies but has rendered them politically minoritarian and somehow silent.

Q. *Oligarchies as defined thus exist both in democratic and in non-democratic societies.*

A. In the former, they emerge in an explicit fashion when the majority decides, for example, to implement redistributive policies in response to imminent or current economic crises or, as happens in the initial phase of constructing democracy, in order to rebalance equalities of opportunity in the enjoyment of primary goods, as, for example, health or education, thereby resisting the creation of conditions for democratic citizenship.

In periods of economic expansion, the oligarchies are politically invisible because they do not need to enter the game, insofar as general prosperity alone is enough to keep the majority in check, so to speak. Full employment makes the "many" able to tax themselves and finance the social politics they decide to implement. But at critical moments, when the democratic state (which is, we should not forget, a government of the greatest number and therefore of the less prosperous also) intervenes in order to confront the emergency, the "many-few" dialectic acquires a very obvious socioeconomic valency—and the outcome of the vote counting is not only the political majority and minority. When the majority is inclined to seek out more resources and threatens to mount an attack on "big money," for example, through fiscal policies, the social sectors in which the money is most heavily concentrated manifest a certain edginess, become visible and unsheathe their weapons, starting with the creation of parties explicitly hostile to taxation or with the identification of leaders dedicated to defending their interests and to resisting social policies through the power of ideology and of the law. The Italian economist Luciano Gallino has provided a very convincing explanation of this phenomenon in a number of his recent publications, documenting the success of the neoliberal ideology against social-liberal or social-democratic ideology from the end of the 1970s onward.

The decline of general prosperity linked to economic crises tends to engender two opposed phenomena: on the one hand, the denunciation of growing inequality (hence the slogan "Occupy Wall Street"), and, on the other, a resistance to equality. In circumstances of impoverishment, Aristotle teaches us, it seems that the few no longer manage to live as equals amid the many without running the risk of seeing their wealth reduced. There is then a backlash that in some historical contexts has been tragic: we should recall in this regard the Chilean coup of 1973 against the democratically elected President Salvador Allende, which used violence to curtail social policies and imposed a radical shift toward the free market. That tragic event inaugurated throughout Latin America a long period of antidemocratic policies associated with free-market projects.

Q. You certainly do not mean to compare the current situation with that of the Chile of Allende and of General Augusto Pinochet.

A. The reference to oligarchies enables me to point to a shift in perspective. I do not want to seem alarmist, still less to suggest catastrophic scenarios. I use those historical examples to try to demonstrate my thesis. As Adam Przeworski has written in his seminal work on democracy and the market, social classes exist and act to reinforce the power they already possess—or, if they do not possess it, to acquire the political power with which to boost their own bargaining position with regard to the rival class, or to protect their own prerogatives better, or to improve their own circumstances. The "many" arm themselves with political power as the most effective strategy for curbing the social power of the oligarchical class, not being able on their own account to call upon sufficient economic and social forces. The strength of the less prosperous class, or of the "many," can only be the union of strengths, that is, number. This is what generations of political thinkers, from Aristotle to Marx, teach us; this is what the writings of contemporary theorists like Przeworski and Larry Diamond remind us.

Q. Przeworski has concentrated upon certain dilemmas faced by workers' parties in the democratic process. Diamond, for his part, has always insisted upon the need for an improvement in the mechanisms of democracy before it can be successfully spread across the world. What link is there between these two authors and the slogan of "the 1 percent" used by the Occupy Wall Street militants?

A. In their different ways Przeworski and Diamond have explained how, in recent years, there has been an escalation of inequality in all countries with mature democracies and how, as a consequence, democratic governments have sought to respond by implementing redistributive policies through fiscal instruments. This is where the change in the role of oligarchies comes in, as they endeavor to block attempts to tax financial revenues, curb the privileges of the banks, or increase fiscal quotas for the very rich. At the same time, everyday hardship, the loss of jobs and very often of housing also, lead an even higher proportion of the "many" to feel ever less tolerant toward the excessive economic power of those who have been defined, symbolically, as the 1 percent. The "few" and the "many" become more visible and, in addition, less inclined to compromise and therefore more radical in their stances.

Q. What is the problem for democracy? Have we not said that, being a political and not an economic system, democracy does not impose economic equality?

A. For democracy the problem is not wealth as such but its concentration, because it can easily lead whoever enjoys it to seek to dominate the political sphere, the power to make laws that all must obey. The iron grip the oligarchies have on the financial markets constitutes a challenge to the sovereignty of states, and democratic states in particular.

Q. How, from a theoretical point of view, can the relations between equality and democracy be summarized?

A. What type of equality is democratic equality? First of all, it is of a political and legal nature as well as being, as I argued earlier, of a moral nature: we should be, and are declared, all equal before the law and in our statutory right to vote, and we are likewise equal in civil rights, or as persons who seek to be treated with equal dignity and respect. This political form of equality is of the utmost importance: in a democracy, the vote of every citizen must count as one vote regardless of that citizen's social, cultural, or economic specificity, in other words, regardless of the weight of money, the strength of that citizen's reputation, and the broadness of that citizen's social connections. One head, one vote: this is the revolutionary norm of democracy. It is revolutionary because it deliberately disregards nonpolitical differences and even inequalities at the moment of making decisions (or of voting for a specific candidate or of approving laws in parliament). In the course of its history, democracy has agreed to endorse and has even created systems of juridical supervision in order to prevent the majority (the governing force) from violating these universal rights. In short, the procedural system of democratic decision making is based upon the following premise: the creation of an artificial identity—citizenship—that is autonomous and separate from other social identities; every citizen has the same entry visa to the political sphere, regardless of the "substance" of their identities. This is the principle, actually the norm, of democracy; this is what makes it a political order of lawmaking.

I would like to insist upon this point. We are not concerned here with equality of possessions or of wealth but with equal conditions as regards competing for public posts, equal treatment by the law, and an equal political voice (the vote, freedom of speech and of association, in order to be able to compete on an equal footing in the formation of a majority and of public opinion). This is the essence of democratic citizenship.

Q. It would be helpful if, at this juncture, you were to take a step backward in time, returning to the Greek thinkers, who were the first really to address such issues.

A. In a fragment attributed to Solon, we read that the law must protect itself from wealth by preventing economic power from acquiring the power to decide the laws. Democracy therefore was born as a compromise between the "many" (that is, the common people composing the middle and poorer classes) and the powerful, who are always numerically few, as Aristotle wrote. In addition, Aristotle explains, democracy was born as a reaction not to the condition of poverty but to the reduction of the poor to slavery because of their indebtedness to the rich. The problem of democracy, then, is not poverty in and by itself but the domination and suppression of liberty that poverty can create. Poverty is a problem because it obstructs or threatens liberty. The link democracy presumes between social condition and political liberty lies here, in so far as it makes us understand why this political order cannot be indifferent to the social and economic condition in which its citizens live. The legal and institutional organization cannot fulfill the promise of political equality. Democracy is a theory of liberty by means of political equality, a power that allows citizens to intervene, if need be, in social and economic life. The most exemplary democratic society of antiquity was born of the revolt of the Athenian many reduced to servitude by the few and when under an obligation to repay the debts they had contracted. Solon's first act was the cancellation of debts. The correlated and subsequent acts were the introduction of *isonomia*, or the legal and political equality of all Athenians, and then of *isegoria*, or the equal opportunity to speak in the assembly. Two liberties, in short, were involved in the emancipation from servitude: that of participating actively, or with the vote, and that of participating with the voice, or in order to determine the political will of the city. Democracy was born in order to render those who were different in something (wealth) equal in their public relationships and in political power. This was designed to give the greater number the strength to resist the economic power of the few and to guarantee their liberty and that of the city; democracy therefore promised liberty and social peace. Although contemporary democracy is very different from the ancient kind and actually implemented through representation rather than direct lawmaking by the citizens, this individualistic foundation of political identity has not changed.

The eradication of debts and of slavery: herein lies the origin of the government of the *demos*, which represents the basic will not to consent to poverty, not solely because of deprivation of material goods but more importantly because it was seen as the main cause of humiliation and servitude. Democracy is the assertion of liberty and individual respect through the creation of a symbolic dimension, which is artificial and constituted by a law that promises to be equal for all and by the possibility of all citizens participating in the construction of the laws.

Q. *In the history of Athens it was not so much the reforms of Solon as those of Cleisthenes that shifted the city toward democracy.*

A. The revolution that bears Cleisthenes' name put a halt to economic and social conflicts by turning them into political conflicts, as it were. It reconfigured the *demoi* by distributing public functions without heeding class or social identity but rather by effecting a numerical redivision of the quarters and of the circumscriptions from which lots were drawn for magistrates. In this way it created a field of conflict and of public interaction distinct from the economic, social, and religious spheres, upon which specifications of class or identity were supposed no longer to have any direct purchase. How then did Cleisthenes differ from Solon? Solon intervened directly in the system of debts in order to free the Athenians and put an end to the social wars; Cleisthenes redesigned the procedures and the geoinstitutional system, with a view to creating a tier of decision making that transcended the membership of classes and families, thereby prefiguring a public space in which the actors were individual citizens. Cleisthenes' reform was not designed to eliminate the differences between social classes, but it used a new instrument of social pacification to annul the political power of those differences, namely, political procedures and institutions. It wrenched individuals—so far as their decision-making capacities were concerned—from their niches of caste membership and group solidarity. It created a new homogeneous space based upon residence, in which individuals-citizens who were equal in something—not in everything—could function and who, by dint of this new equality, could run the city's public business without strife. There then occurred the passage from ascriptive statuses or memberships to roles acquired through direct doing and by choice.

Q. Cleisthenes turned each Athenian into a "hyphenated individual," as we would put it today, in the sense that he enabled each of them to be a part of a group: to enjoy a social status and to be also at the same time equal to everyone else.

A. The notion of *isonomia* contains the idea of this revolutionary shift, which has had a momentous impact upon Western political history, transforming the political dimension into a symbolic and normative one and freeing it from force and brute power. *Isonomia* already existed, but through Cleisthenes it was transformed: if previously it had been claimed by those few oligarchs who were struggling against the power of the tyrant, from then on it took a new direction: equality extended to the nonequals created a dimension that transcended the social and ethical dimension of wealth and virtue. I would like to use Jean-Pierre Vernant's words to explain this novelty, that is to say, the birth at one and the same time of politics and of democracy. By contrast with political communities that are nondemocratic, in which in times of crisis people appeal to a person described as having special gifts (like an oracle or a tyrant), a democratic city relies upon the ideal of *isonomia*, which entails that the people resolve their problems through the normal functioning of political institutions they have made. In detaching him from clan and family, Athenian democracy created a citizen with the power to vote: an individual who was placed in a circumstance such that he could think and reflect upon the questions that the community proposed to confront, and he did this as an inhabitant of a *demos* of the city, not as a private person and not even as the member of a class (as was the case with the oligarchs). In emancipating themselves from the arbitrary power of the few, the *demos* was able to create an artificial domain open to all, also to the few.

Q. You seem to reckon that the meaning of Cleisthenes' revolution has become paradigmatic. Can you explain in more detail why?

A. Cleisthenes constructed a kind of unified civic space within which the Athenians, regardless of their family, profession, and even of their virtue and knowledge, could operate as equivalent one to the other by dint of their being citizens of the same *polis*. The democratic *polis* is a universe without a "below" or an "above," without hierarchical levels: its geometrical form is the circle. If it is true that Cleisthenes did not discredit wealth or economic power, it is also true that in his political system wealth could be discredited in the act of making a decision inasmuch as it had been detached from the fact of belonging to a class: the individual Athenian became nonetheless a protagonist of political decision making. Rendering the individual central to democracy was a strategy designed to bolster those who were essentially only individuals and could not rely upon social connections and strong classes like the nobles or the oligarchs.

In democracy, the individual, becoming a citizen, makes himself a protagonist whereas collective identities and groups decline. This is the meaning of the individualist character of political equality. It is the locus of its power but is also its weakness because the only weapon it has on its side is the vote and the voice. Herein lies the enduring value of this political form. In remodeling the *polis*—Vernant explained—Cleisthenes followed an ideal of "the egalitarian city" in which all the citizens were "on the same plane," or occupied, in relation to a common center, "symmetrical and reversible positions." The values of equality appeared in Athens to be all the more accentuated inasmuch as the citizens remedied a state of affairs whose hallmark was separation and division, namely, membership in local clienteles. Thus with political equality they achieved both freedom and unifying peace.

The aim of *isonomia* is to reconstitute and consolidate the unity of the civic body, or to restore peace to the community. In Athens, isonomic democracy was meant to end civil war and radical disagreement. It was meant to unite the citizens by guaranteeing them equal access to political power, that is, the liberty to make decisions. It did it not by suppressing or negating social differences, nor by uprooting them or compartmentalizing them (as Plato, for example, proposed in *The Republic*, where indeed he separated those concerned with production from those concerned with government, making politics a function restricted to only some and turning politicians into a caste of guardians separated from society), but by having them interact on a plane open to and equal for all, namely, that of public functions.

Isonomia was not intended to suppress social antagonisms, nor to eliminate conflicts, but to transfer them to another plane, namely, politics, which became thus the name of an art practiced by the citizens and based on speech, voting, and the collective interaction of the participants in public space. Democracy creates the possibility of peace in liberty through an open space of words within which political equality lives. As a consequence, it is fair to say that democracy endures so long as neither poverty nor wealth enter directly into the political game, influencing rules and decisions, indeed, determining them thanks to the exorbitant use that the few and the many can always make of power: the former with privilege and oppression and the latter with the strength of numbers or the threat of rebellion. Athens was therefore a democracy when and for so long as it sought to sunder economic power from political power and in addition when it adopted procedures that regulated (and thus limited) the power of the assembly without undermining it.

Q. Suppose we advance a couple of millennia: the advent of capitalism highlighted a new dialectic between economic power and the requirements of democracy, which has been transformed over time and undergone an oscillation over the years, especially during the twentieth century, but which nonetheless provides a key to interpreting the mutation we are discussing.

A. The compromise between capitalism and democracy has been made possible by the compromise between the private ownership of the means of production and universal suffrage: because those owning the former (a minority) have been prepared to live under political institutions in which decisions were the outcome of the aggregate of the votes of everyone, or of both the few and the many, counted according to the rule of majority (therefore favoring the many). The holders of economic power have accepted the democratic risk: this is the sense of the compromise between capitalism and democracy. Admittedly, their acceptance was out of an instrumental calculation, since number is a deterrent force that the few would prefer to have as friendly as possible. If the few are subject to a government whose power is exercised by the force of number (thus not their force), it is because they know they can trust the many. In Thomas Hobbes's logic, the threatening force of the many was a condition that induced the few to stay in the democratic game. To come to our topic: in order for that compromise to hold, it was necessary that the many did not live in conditions of poverty and not nurse resentment toward those who had more, since this could lead them to use the rule of majority as an instrument of punishment and revenge against them. The government of the majority would open the door to instability and social unrest. To neutralize this risk, it has been historically necessary, as in Solonian Athens, to release the poor from their economic subjection to the rich, thus making them a force for stability. Just as Solon cancelled the debts and freed the debtors from the yoke of rule by their masters, so too in twentieth-century democracy the many were freed from the scourge of poverty through the non-aleatory possibility of working. Rendering them economically capable of taking care of themselves and their children has by the same token restored their dignity. Opening the door to general prosperity, it has become possible to achieve a compromise between those who owned the means of production and those who essentially owned only their own physical strength. The force of number therefore had a deterrent function of peace rather than being a factor of violent conflict and war. This was the answer to the challenge thrown down by Hobbes and by Marx: a challenge that is not exotic and ideological—indeed, precisely the reverse.

Q. *Keynesianism has sought to provide an answer to this challenge, hasn't it?*

A. Yes, establishing the ideological foundations of and the political justifications for this compromise, which emerged in response to the crisis of 1929 and to the catastrophic impoverishment that followed it and that led to war. In that period, politics extended its decision-making competence beyond the classical sphere—public order and defense against external enemies—in order to intervene in the economic sphere and in the social relationship between the classes. The compromise between capitalism and democracy was possible because the rules of the game assigned to the state a central role in the solution to the problem of impoverishment and therefore to that of the distribution of opportunities. Equal access to careers and a right to education and training, and then access to the possibility of being cured: full-employment politics, access to schooling, and the right to health were the first major public interventions implemented by European democracies after World War II, intended not so much to mitigate economic differences as to neutralize them in order to boost citizenship.

Instead of assisting the poor, as the liberal state had done in the decades preceding the Great Depression, the state now promoted social policies that generated employment through ambitious public works programs and services that guaranteed social security. By thus creating the conditions for work, the state favored democracy: once again, as in antiquity, it emancipated from the servitude of need by creating democratic citizenship. The latter, though it does not abolish private property nor pursue equality of wealth, does however demand that social conditions not be those of indigence and servile dependence on oligarchies old and new. The goal is freedom, and social redistribution is the means to achieve it.

Q. What role did economic doctrine play in that tricky transitional phase?

A. Democracy started its journey in the twentieth century when the paradigm of laissez-faire and of nonintervention by the state was put in question. To mention just two figures centrally involved in that old ideological dispute, consider Herbert Spencer, the spokesman of social Darwinism and of moral and economic laissez-faire, and by contrast Leonard Hobhouse, who in the early years of the twentieth century espoused a liberalism that championed social rights—first and foremost, the right to work—and endorsed the idea of social responsibility toward individuals. Against Spencer, to whom is owed the first organic ideological construction of a free-market philosophy, the social and economic philosophy that emerged from World War I mobilized the state as a means to distribute resources and opportunities, even before serving as a means to include the beneficiaries in citizenship. The outcome would not be socialism or the Spartan egalitarianism preached by communism but a major endeavor of wealth creation fueled by work and consumption, upon which the electoral suffrage would have conferred political validity. Increase in demand became the flywheel of employment and of growth—and also of citizenship.

Q. A compromise, then, that turned out to suit both the "few" and the "many" . . .

A. Upon this reciprocal convenience was consolidated the social contract that rendered constitutional democracy possible in the aftermath of World War II. The reason is not hard to find, since the contract of citizenship was founded upon work, that is, upon the extension of the taxable base and upon the possibility of the state implementing fiscal policies with which to fund public works and to finance public services. The circle work-taxation-services was the backbone of democratic citizenship. As Léon Blum said, better distribution can revitalize employment and at the same time satisfy the need for stability and social justice. Work and citizenship could march in step. This meant, on the one hand, that democracy would not level private property but would enable the greatest possible number of persons to make a dignified life for themselves through work; on the other hand, it meant that democracy was possible precisely because citizenship was founded upon paid labor.

Q. *You have cited Blum, who was prime minister in France before and after World War II? What about Italy?*

A. The preamble to the Italian constitution renders perfectly the meaning of the social pact when it affirms that Italy is "a republic founded on work," or that political liberty is possible because citizens are socially autonomous, not dependent on bosses nor public charity. Once born, democratic citizenship launched an ambitious campaign against poverty, which became an ill not to be mitigated but to be uprooted. Poverty was given a precise name: *unemployment,* the lack of work. The entire democratic system was sustained by the possibility each had to take care of himself and to look after his children. And to do so with dignity and by means of an activity that did not humiliate, namely, work in return for a decent wage.

Treating work as the foundation of the political system entails revising its value and meaning: it signifies freeing it from the stigma of subjection and making it a condition of possibility and autonomy. This is a Herculean task that modern democracy has only completed in part and with difficulty. We should not forget, in this regard, that the Nazi and Fascist regimes themselves took their bearings from work, and this is another reason why those political philosophers who sought to put the liberty of the person at the center felt it incumbent upon themselves to oppose work-worshipping philosophies. Work made persons free because it enabled them to be political protagonists.

Consider, for example, the case of Hannah Arendt, who opposes "activity" to "work" as creation and natality to reproduction and necessity. Besides, the classical philosophical tradition was unanimous in presenting work as the opposite of liberty: the ancients' critique of democracy reflected this conception: as we have noted, democracy was the government of the poor and of those who lived by toil. But for we moderns democracy is the rule of all because the rule of a society of individuals who assume direct responsibility for themselves, not individuals living parasitically off rents, nor off the exploitation of others, nor even living, as the ancients did, off the work of slaves.

As explained by Max Weber, the moderns have adapted democracy to market society and wage labor. This is a society, based on consumption, that does not want a mass of poor people but one of consumers, that is, of people neither too rich nor too poor, and therefore with needs to satisfy. The moderns have promoted a fundamental transformation from which the history of our democratic citizenship may be held to have begun: the end of servile labor and of slavery.

The concepts of work, political equality, and individual liberty are closely interconnected, each of them being based on the notion that the individual is the primary good: an enterprising and active person who sees in work a means not only to satisfy primary material needs but also to express his or her own talents and capabilities, and finally a sign of responsibility toward his or her life that the society must respect and sustain through a system of rights. The dignity of the person and a dignified labor have given rise to the ethical world of modern democracies, a world in which needs and rights are intertwined. In this respect, the moderns are superior to the ancients.

Q. However, we cannot in good faith maintain that this association between work and political equality has eliminated injustices or freed work from the burden of necessity.

A. That is true, but it has helped us view the difficulty of living as a condition that can be humanized though never overcome. Having political rights has helped us treat work as a social condition subject to rules and to reciprocal and shared responsibilities. The latter half of the twentieth century has given a concrete demonstration of the humanizing effects of democracy in the world of work. The data uncovered by those political scientists who study the processes of democratization demonstrate that the democratic transformation brings social, economic, and cultural betterment: more dignified working conditions, the right to welfare assistance and insurance contributions, social services for families and decent public schools. We are led to conclude that, if this is true for recently democratized societies, such as several countries in Latin America, it will be still more so for those with an established democracy. Yet the democracy-prosperity paradigm does not really appear to be set in stone, and a thing that may hold true for the younger democratic societies does not hold good in societies like ours, where two troubling phenomena have in fact manifested themselves in recent years, namely, a decline in the regulation of the work relationship and of the rights linked to work, such as social security or protection against unemployment and the growth of poverty. As the figures impress upon us virtually every day, workplace accidents are in Italy more frequent now than they were some years ago. Working conditions are less safe either because they are less strictly regulated or because they are not regulated at all. It is reasonable to say that work disassociated from the guarantees of safety is the mirror image of a society in which work is no longer thought in terms of rights but has reverted to being simply sacrifice and mere toil. Work disassociated from a range of basic certainties, work placed in the frame of risk rather than in that of opportunities, tends to change its identity in the imaginary or in public opinion: from being a condition associated with rights and dignity, it becomes a place of mounting social inequalities and of the fear of poverty. What is then jeopardized is precisely the relationship between work and political autonomy, which is in fact the condition of modern democratic citizenship. I hold it to be a very worrying sign of the social and cultural distress of our established democracies.

Q. *In this framework, the crux of poverty takes on a very different connotation.*

A. Poverty requires serious thought, but not so as to legalize it through a system of public and private charity interventions like food stamps or various sorts of "welfare cards" (which the Italian government put into effect in the summer of 2008). Poverty is a word that somehow conceals or masks the problem of powerlessness and the decline of rights and security. At the heart of switching vocabulary from exploitation to poverty, there is the changed relationship between work and rights. Poverty is accompanied by a decline in social rights, which actually entails an erosion of the political efficacy of citizenship for an increasing number of citizens. Short-term contracts often pave the way to future poverty. Work without rights is a passport to destitution. The present has just as many risks, not only because there is an objective diminution in employment opportunities but also because of the practice of accepting work without rights, work for the present, without any assurances for the future. Propaganda against tenured jobs—for the most part orchestrated by those who, like university professors and economists, already have them—leaves one speechless. As we know, ideologies help us swallow bitter pills. Nonetheless, there is something truly striking about the unanimity displayed by these praise-singers of precarious work and the freedom to fire without the slightest justification. Today workers are more vulnerable and weaker but also readier to barter their freedom and safety for a few pennies. And the tendency to disassociate work and rights leads us to associate work with some kind of toil. This is, at one and the same time, a sign and a premonition of the greatest fear of all, namely, poverty.

Poverty breeds shame. In a society in which consumption is the ordinary paradigm of self-representation and of successful relationships with others, failing to own specific goods is equivalent to feeling oneself actually to have failed and to have become marginalized. Poverty is a stigma worse than ill-paid work, worse than work without rights. Better to be slaves than to be without social recognition. You can understand why it should be so, since, in a society sustained by the condition of equality (which induces a comparative frame of the mind), not enjoying equal consideration (it does not matter in relation to what) engenders humiliation and resentment. These latter are unbearable emotions because, while they do not alter the circumstances of the person suffering them for the better, they prevent the growth of other emotions such as empathy and solidarity, which are essential to a democratic society. This is the reason why the association of work with rights not only cannot be regarded as "optional," or as an alternative that one could as easily do without, but is to all intents and purposes a factor in democratic stability.

Q. Reverting to what we were discussing earlier, can we say that after the collapse of the compromise between democracy and capital-

ism the poor will become the representatives of the general interests of society?

A. Their emancipation paved the way for the emancipation of all the subaltern classes and above all blocked the restorational policies sustained by the class that held economic power, which resisted state intervention in the economy and in labor relationships. If the property-owning class was prepared to come to terms with the working classes, it was not out of generosity or moral sentiment. This agreement suited the few because the broadening of consumption set in motion production and the most important investment, that of social concord, to which the name "citizenship" was given. A twin-track policy—full employment and political equality—represented the foundation of the democratic constitutions after World War II and was also the reason why the political parties became key protagonists.

Q. *Can you explain just what the role of the parties was in the allocation of economic resources?*

A. The policy of employment and of the distribution of social goods and services was implemented by party democracy: political parties were collective forces that managed the electoral process and the selection of the political class, and that at the same time created a buffer zone between economic classes and the state, thus filtering interests and preventing them from capturing the state. The parties assumed responsibility for managing the programs and representing the social forces, which in their turn were prepared not to intervene autonomously. The parties became the "intermediate bodies" of modern democracy, the equivalents of the social intermediate bodies that Montesquieu had recognized as essential to the moderation and stability of government. These new intermediate bodies—the political parties—were peculiar to democratic society: in Tocqueville's terms, they were consistent with the two principles upon which democratic society rests, namely, equality and voluntary participation. The political parties are free associations that citizens create in order to compete and to implement their own projects. In the aftermath of World War II, when constitutional democracy signed the compromise between capital and labor, they became the actors that put the social classes in the back row and that took on the task of mediating between the opposed interests, making decisions that would as far as possible reflect a broader interest.

Q. Aside from the role of the parties, how has this compromise evolved in the recent history of the European democracies?

A. In Europe, and certainly Italy, democratic society was born from the ashes of World War II. It was born out of the material need for reconstruction and the moral need to vaccinate the political system in order to prevent a relapse into solutions involving tyranny or collective impoverishment. It was an extraordinary ideal and material project, firmly rooted, and not only in procedures and institutions. And in this process the culture of solidarity was not altogether a secondary factor. In Great Britain the Labour government of Clement Attlee, coming into office after defeating Winston Churchill's Conservatives, decided to implement a package of welfare reforms outlined a few years earlier in a report drafted by the economist and sociologist William Beveridge. It was a reconstruction plan that rested upon two pillars, one political and the other social, with at its heart the idea that, in order to enjoy citizenship or to be equal in the political sphere, citizens needed social opportunities, effective capabilities that education, social relationships, and health provide. Without public interventions in these spheres, citizens would never be able to compete in politics from a position of equality. Social democracy has therefore replied to Marx by rendering public some nonpublic goods and in this fashion has extended the sphere of political decision making. Rather than abolishing the state, social democracy made the state a primary actor of social justice. This is why the states of Western Europe, Italy among them, were in fact born out of social-democratic projects (even where, as in Italy, those projects were represented and implemented by a Catholic party rather than a social-democratic party): not by chance, as I remarked above, the Italian constitution declares Italy to be a republic founded upon work, which implies a commitment by the state to foster employment. Today, indeed, work is the most fiercely contested battleground because the attempt is being made to tie it to the rules of the market and to free it from political and juridical regulation. The trajectory is to make all economic relationships, including work, depoliticized.

Q. You maintain that the compromise between democracy and capitalism has been shattered, paving the way to the antiegalitarian mutation and even to repercussions for the functioning of the political parties.

A. It seems to me that the classes have taken in hand again the decision-making power, not all the classes but particularly the class that holds the economic wealth, which is now not only the means of production but above all the financial revenues. In Keynesian terms, the compromise between capital and labor could work because capital accumulation fueled new investments and the widening of consumption. From the 1980s, a novel doctrine began to gain ground: the very same doctrine that diagnosed the end of ideologies and declared the rules of the market to be norms that were as natural and as fatal as those that explained the motion of heavenly bodies in terms of their submitting to the law of gravity. Society as a whole can regulate itself, it was thus argued, without the intervention of politically made law; indeed, it can better distribute costs and benefits, according to merit and need, precisely because it does it with the voluntary collaboration of individuals instead of through the imposition of government plans of distributive justice. This shift bears the names of two leaders, Margaret Thatcher and Ronald Reagan, and has proved strangely alluring even in the university world, shaping generations of theorists and economists, financial experts and "reprogrammers" of social policy. Neoliberal thought set out to advance an antistate ideology that would attract consensus around the idea that curtailing policies of redistribution and social justice would help inject new energy and entrepreneurial freedom into the system. It mobilized less against Soviet socialism than against Western social democracy, a political project vested with a great deal of legitimacy in the first decades after World War II. The new free-market doctrine rose up against social interpretations of democracy, therefore first of all against the perspectives opened up by the Beveridge Plan and the reconstruction ambitions of T. H. Marshall and, in the United States, against the plan of Lyndon B. Johnson or the theory of justice proposed by John Rawls.

Q. Thatcherism and Reaganomics, that is to say, the economic policy of the Reagan period inspired by Milton Friedman, Arthur Laffer, and the Chicago School, pointed the finger at taxation . . .

A. . . . which was, in that period, the mechanism democracy had used to stabilize itself. The new doctrine assailed taxes both from the point of view of political ideology and from that of economic appropriateness.

In the former case, taxes were criticized from an individualist perspective: as work the individual is forced to do for the state, fueling a swollen bureaucracy that removes the decision as to how to invest resources from those who create those selfsame resources.

The restriction upon politics, its withdrawal from the economic sphere, is here a condition of social peace and the foundation of the sentiment of justice because, neoliberals argue, the market distributes according to impersonal and unpolitical criteria. Hence the idea of a liberal justice that is noninterventionist and that, Robert Nozick maintained, operates according to the maxim "From each as they choose, to each as they are chosen." Let's cite from Nozick's *Anarchy, State, and Utopia* of 1974: To maintain a "distributional patterned principle of justice" over time, "one must either interfere continually to stop people from transferring resources as they wish to, or continually (or periodically) interfere to take from some persons resources that others for some reason choose to transfer to them." In conclusion, "no distributional patterned principle of justice can be continuously realized without continuous interference with people's life" and compelling them to do what perhaps they would otherwise never do.

Nozick was right: a democratic society that seeks to preserve a level of social well-being that is widespread among the many has to intervene in social and economic relationships. If at the center of public concern there is not a simple paradigm but the concrete circumstance of men and women that make choices and have expectations of recognition, the problem will then probably concern the forms of interference rather than the choice between interference and noninterference. Political interventions, as Martha Nussbaum and Amartya Sen have argued, may be multiple, assuming the form both of universalistic redistributive policies and of actions that are indirect, that are in the guise of incentives and are framed in response to needs. The difference between the former and the latter stems from the attention paid by politics and economics to the concrete situation in which citizens happen to live, the prejudices and values within which is encapsulated their freedom of choice, and the social and cultural difficulties that are interposed between the equality of principle of which they are the titulars (fundamental rights), or the potentiality to make meaningful choices, and the effects these choices have upon their personal life and relationships.

The "warning" issued by Sen to the economy was that it not transform itself from a "social science" into a "science of nature" and that it regard the pursuit of well-being as a commitment to attaining a condition of life that is dignified.

The judgment on the forms of intervention is therefore a judgment on means and their greater or lesser efficacy relative to the circumstances and conditions prevailing in a given society. The goal is to consider the individual as a social actor and a person worthy of equal respect. As Sen clarified when amending the neoliberal paradigm, we should go beyond economic growth to understand the broader implications of development and of the pursuit of social welfare. Democratic societies should pay attention to the extensive evidence that political and civil rights tend to enhance freedoms of other kinds (such as human security) through giving a voice, at least in many circumstances, to the deprived and the vulnerable. Economic independence, as John Stuart Mill maintained more than a century and a half ago, is a corollary of liberty and, as such, justifies the interference of the state and a transformation of the legislation that regulates the social relations of property in order to "rectify" everything that "conflicts" with "the ends which render private property" compatible with its own principle, which is that of guaranteeing "to individuals the fruits of their own labour and abstinence."

Neoliberal philosophy and ideology militated against this view and was able to obtain political consent for a cause that was, paradoxically enough, not in the interest of the many! The prevailing ideology is that increasing taxes is not only a form of slavery, and one that deprives individuals of the opportunity to make choices and run risks, but is also an open door to a bureaucratic monster, the social-welfare state, which while it sucks social energies, engenders dysfunctional and inefficient services. Underneath this social theory there is the idea that civil servants or politicians know much less than do individuals about what is in their (individuals') interests because the state and the people have divergent interests, so that what suits it does not suit them. Besides, redistributive policies are consecrated, or so it was claimed, to increase; they therefore bear within themselves the germ of despotism because they cannot decide to change down without jeopardizing the entire system of social justice. This ideology may be highly attractive to liberals and democrats, as indeed it proved to be, because it uses very astutely the argument of antityranny: social-democratic policies—neoliberals argue—are inexorably headed, unless checked and interrupted, toward antiliberal forms of government. And since they do not have the capacity to be self-limiting—because to persist they need to expand—it is necessary to stop them altogether by blocking their source at its origin, namely, taxation. Policies of tax reduction are policies of liberty because they are antiauthoritarian: such, in essence, is the alluring theoretical kernel of the free marketeers' assault upon social democracy. This ideology has had a doubly decisive role, in that it has cunningly shifted the antagonism between social classes onto the relationships between state and individual: the real enemies of the workers, according to this logic, are not the owners of the means of production or the system of exploitation that capitalism implies. The real antagonism is the one between the taxpayers and the bureaucrats, a ravenous new feudal class that lives off those who produce and has interests diametrically opposed to those who produce.

From circa the 1980s onward, war was therefore waged against a welfare state that "leeches" off citizens, taxing them with the promise of redistributing resources. If society were to claw back the power to decide upon the allocation of the resources that it produces—the ideologues of deregulation insisted—it would gain in dynamism, development, and justice, as well as in freedom. Consequently neoliberalism formulated an antitax philosophy and strategy, its motivation being that, apart from responding to calls for economic freedom and respect for basic rights (first and foremost property rights), it would enable greater growth, restoring to the economy resources confiscated by the state through taxation and often squandered on wasteful projects.

The slashing of taxes, which in reality was more marked in the United States and Great Britain than in continental Europe or Italy, has not brought about a homogeneous growth of society but a more unequal society and an unequal development. Social inequality has visibly increased in the last thirty years, as Thomas Piketty proved very effectively. We have witnessed a redistribution of resources and opportunities favoring the collectors of profits, the justification being that this would serve to stimulate investments. Yet instead of freeing resources for productive investment, the cutting of taxes has given free rein to the accumulation of financial revenues.

Q. *What effects is the breach of the social compromise having on the political parties?*

A. Some claim that the crisis of the parties had its origin in political factors such as, for example, the decline of the ideologies and thus of party membership. This can't be denied. But these phenomena of the erosion of the "intermediate bodies" of postwar representative democracy seem to be a consequence rather than the cause of the breach of the compromise upon which democracy had been founded after World War II. The crisis of the parties is the mirror image of a society that has witnessed the end of a cycle in which the state saw to the emancipation of the oppressed classes in return for their cooperation in the social enterprise. Now it is the "other" class—the one that holds the power to influence society by relying upon labor as a resource—that directly manages its own interests. The decline of full-employment politics represents an admission that compromise between capitalism and democracy can be interrupted or violated. There is no need to reawaken Marx in order to register these changes; the diagnosis is within everyone's reach. This too is the great mutation of our times.

5

The Secession from Democracy

*Q. Living and working in Manhattan, a few kilometers away from the
eye of the financial cyclone, you have been an eyewitness to a crisis that
has not only accentuated the ravages of a free-market doctrine without
rules but has also had a violent impact upon the culture, upon access to
information, and upon the lives of millions of savers.*

A. I remember the effect that reading the *New York Times* had on
me in the months when the financial crisis was only a year and a half
old, when the cures proposed by governments and financial experts
did not appear to be wholly appropriate. It was October–November
2009: one year after the historic and rapturously received election of
Barack Obama to the White House, the most turbulent phase of the
financial storm. In those weeks, the American daily gave the impression of being a compendium of extracts from the *Communist Manifesto*. Everyone from lawyers in Paris to the workers without rights in
Beijing, the journalists in the *New York Times* recounted, stood watch-
ing, powerless and terrified, as jobs disappeared and the value of port-
folios plummeted. Like a world war, the recession was global. It was
just as global, in fact, as financial capitalism, and no one was immune
to the risks of bankruptcy: neither the big banks nor the small investors
who could not manage to pay their mortgages. There did not seem to
be any remedy. Economic experts were bolder in describing the crisis,
often depicting it in apocalyptic terms, than they were in suggesting

solutions. They too seemed to have become acquainted with Marx and Engels's text. In the fall of 2009, Director of National Intelligence Dennis C. Blair informed the U.S. Congress that the instability occasioned by the economic crisis would prove to be in the years ahead—for they were already talking of years and not just of months—the greatest threat the country would have to face since the attacks of September 2001. In short, the economic crisis was more akin to terrorism than to war: a threat unpredictable in its effects and its duration, impossible to dominate or safely to combat. Two years later, in September 2011, there erupted the Occupy Wall Street movement, a short distance away from the chasm left by the conflagration that ten years before had destroyed the World Trade Center. Yet the crisis was neither neutral nor impartial in its effects; it did not affect people randomly or in proportion to their lack of information and prudence. As a matter of fact, the crisis produced something like a selection: some (the many) would be impoverished while some others (the very few) would increase their wealth. Concerning the United States, data from the Census Bureau and the Internal Revenue Service show that both income and wealth inequality have risen steadily over the past one hundred years or thereabouts—and in correspondence with the cyclical crises. According to the research of Emmanuel Saez and Thomas Piketty, national income inequality has been increasing steadily since the 1970s and has now reached levels not seen since 1928; the data show that the top 1 percent of American earners received nearly 22.5 percent of all pretax income; the bottom 90 percent's share is below 50 percent for the first time since records began. The mean household income for the top 5 percent is almost sixteen times greater than the mean household income for the bottom 10 percent. These trends are not going unnoticed. Pew Research Center surveys from 2012 found that two-thirds of the American public believes there are "very strong" or "strong" conflicts between the rich and the poor—an increase of about 9 percent since 2009—while a full 76 percent agreed with the statement, "it's really true that the rich get richer while the poor get poorer." A similar 2014 survey found that 65 percent of American adults, regardless of their party affiliation, believe that the gap between the rich and everyone else has increased in the last ten years. Americans are well aware of the historically high income differentials they are witnessing, particularly of late, yet very little has been done in the political arena to combat a trend that harms the vast majority of Americans and benefits so few.

Q. *The* New York Times *has claimed for months that the second great depression of the capitalist era had taken everyone unawares. Was this not the case?*

A. Some, very few in number and never heeded, had begun to speak about it years before the collapse of the stock markets, but Reaganite optimism and the boom of the twenty-year-old overnight millionaires in California had perhaps led to their being silenced and branded as communists or as ineffectual Cassandras. Extremist free marketeers had for years spread abroad the "beautiful lie" of the slogan "lower taxes, more prosperity for all," "less regulation, more growth for all," and with popular backing (we should not forget that the free-market ideology was endorsed also by those whom it harmed the most) they had drained public resources in order artificially to create wealth for the few, strewing confetti on the many.

In 1893, Charles Sanders Peirce, the most brilliant and sophisticated of the American pragmatist philosophers, commenting upon the first great wave of free-market ideologies, observed that economics had succeeded in reversing, to its own advantage, the maxim of the Gospel, just as Mandeville had already done in *The Fable of the Bees*: "private vices of every kind are of public benefit," in that by dominating one's neighbor with an economic weapon one ensured the good of both. The economists and financial experts who lord it over the pharaonic business schools on the American campuses—departments that resemble the preservation and propagation office of a monotheistic religious doctrine and that are ceaselessly expanding and attracting students from every continent—have translated this antievangelical maxim into the "trickle-down" formula, that is, a trickling as the topmost basin receiving water from a fountain overflows. According to the free marketeers of the 1980s, the wealth produced in such abundance would stimulate investment and create jobs. The fountain of the wealth of the few would sprinkle little drops of wealth over everyone, and, besides, the effect of detaxation, while it greatly benefited the "few," would also provide some relief to the middle classes and the less prosperous. The philosopher Robert Nozick had completed this train of thought by arguing that paying taxes was equivalent to making oneself a slave and being constrained to give one's own labor to the state. Smashing slavery and winning freedom meant slimming down the state to such an extent that it was forced to concern itself only with its classical functions, repression and the guarding of the borders, that is, the defense of the basic rights (property and life security) from internal and external enemies. The liberalist notion of taxation echoes a conception of the citizen that is opposite to that inaugurated by the republican city-states at the beginning of modernity. Historically, the latter corresponded to pivotal moments in modern democratization, which accompanied the beginning of the process of popular self-determination in modern democracies. As a revolutionary principle, it gave voice to two exigencies that proved to be essential conditions for democratic legitimacy: making the citizens the agents of their own security (handing over the army to the citizens or having the people in the army), interpreting the representative order as derivative of the *droit de cité*, which consists of multiple rights, not only suffrage or the electoral right (the right to free speech, freedom of social and political association, right to petition, right to propose laws, and the right to ask for a referendum on an existing law). Republican citizenship rests on universal taxation. An inclusive and universal taxation was a revolutionary expression of an autonomous citizenry, civil and military. It was not by chance that Machiavelli linked the democratic representative form of the republic (entailing the inclusion of the countryside and of the lower urban classes in the Consiglio Grande) with a progressive taxation and an autonomous army or an army composed of citizens. Taxation was thus not slavery, and in fact it goes together with the controlling power that taxpayers claimed and exercised over the elected or the magistrates in charge of government. "No taxation without representation" did not entail a claim for paying less taxes, but it was a call for achieving political power in determining the agenda and shaping the public affairs of their country. The logic of "trickle down" would seem to imply an effect that was indirect. The allure of this antipublic rhetoric lies in convincing persons that cutting taxes will lead indirectly to a generalized benefit, one without the aid of state planning. Obviously, no one can calculate with precision what happens "indirectly": it is the logic of the system that, like natural providence or by virtue of an invisible, impersonal intelligence, steers in that direction the economic actions of everyone, rich and poor alike, without direct action on the part of the state.

Peirce, who defined himself as a "sentimentalist," had baptized this dogma of modern economics the "gospel of greed." In more recent years, Paul Krugman has spoken of the oligarchy of opulence—which has shaped the opinions of millions of persons in every country of the world using the fable of "trickle down"—as a macroscopic example of greed, which has translated into algorithms and models of problem solving abstractly constructed.

Today it's crystal clear that the droplets of prosperity do not so easily succeed in fostering in the "many" the illusion of having their thirst quenched by spray from the stratospheric profits of the "few." The many—who are not necessarily the most wretched but may well be a part of the middle classes—no longer have the funds to pay the installments owed on their mortgages, and they fear above all losing their jobs. They are almost always fighting among themselves: American or Italian workers against the desperate who arrive from outside to "steal" their jobs.

Q. You therefore see a link with the rise of xenophobia and protectionism.

A. The growth of racism and of violent and intolerant nationalism seems to proceed in proportion to the collapse of the illusion fostered by "trickle down." Both in the United States and in Europe it is the youngest who suffer most from the crisis in employment. Some Western governments see in protectionism the answer to the unemployment of their own citizens: shut your borders to those in search of jobs. We seem to be reading an already familiar story, beginning with the protectionist policies of the liberal states of the end of the nineteenth century and leading to colonialism, militarization, imperialism, and finally the snarling nationalisms of the fascist regimes. The harsh response against the migrants who are knocking at the gates of the First World—but "first" for whom?—seems to round off the plot of an old book. Who will tell the newly impoverished of the "first" world that their enemies are not the "others"? The politics of deregulation and lower taxes has in reality changed the types of accumulation and investment. But the impacts on the national politics of advanced democracies are different.

Certainly the way Americans and Europeans respond to the crisis reveals a very different mentality among the two peoples. Whereas populism and the politics of the closed border is one of the proverbial and still current ideologies in many European countries, American citizens seem to be in the grip of a different mentality. Before answering your question on European public opinion and policies, I would like to inspect the American case. As surveys show, Americans don't actually want anything to be done. While their country has one of the highest ratios of income inequality among advanced countries, only 47 percent of American citizens believe that the gap between the rich and the poor is a major problem. At the height of the Occupy Wall Street movement, in the fall of 2011, reducing the income and wealth gap was low on respondents' list of priorities for government action. Logically, there seems to be a puzzle here. Americans are increasingly aware of income inequality and recognize that this inequality is causing conflict between the rich and the poor. They also appreciate that this is a mounting trend and that there is no indication that the growing difference between the size of the paychecks brought home by the 1 percent and those brought home by everyone else will slow down anytime soon. Yet, say most Americans, nothing should be done. American electors choose to ignore ever-increasing income and wealth gaps, even though current conditions benefit a tiny majority to the detriment of the vast majority. There are many possible interpretations of this laissez-faire mentality so widespread among all social strata of the population and, more specifically, the reality that, according to the most recent survey results of the General Social Survey (GSS), less than half of Americans think the government should act, for example through redistributive taxation, to combat rising income differentials. According to what a student at Columbia University, Margaret Mattes, writes in her thesis, *Understanding the Influence of Class Identity on Policy Opinions Regarding Redistributive Taxation in the United States* (2015), to which I owe most of the information I draw upon in this chapter, it could be that we think the wealthiest are performing a public good through their very existence, inspiring the masses to work hard and serving as philanthropic saviors. It could be that we don't trust the government, the most likely actor, to rectify the situation. It could be that we think the rich deserve exorbitant amounts of wealth. Or it could be that we

fail to recognize a personal or collective common interest in supporting policies that temper inequality. Or that each of us wants to be one
of the wealthiest, those who buy the goods we most desire, live in the
homes of which we dream, and fly first class. Or even that we believe
we will one day fulfill these ambitions. These various explanations are
relevant hypotheses for any critical study of the prevailing mentality of
many American citizens.

This brief overview of the American mentality helps us see the difference in political attitude and culture within the established democracies. The European reaction to the crisis is different, and this difference
derives also from the fact that the democratic reconstruction in the old
continent was made on a promise of social equalization and redistribution of social resources so as to make all citizens capable of satisfying
basic needs that citizenship presumes: schooling, employment, health,
and housing. In continental Europe, democracy and capitalism struck a
compromise on the premise of full employment and redistribution via
taxation. As Adam Przeworski wrote in his book on *Capitalism and
Social Democracy*, "democratic control over the level of unemployment
and the distribution of income became the terms of the compromise
that made democratic capitalism possible" (207). Now, what compromise will democracy be able to reach with this new capitalism, seeking
as it does to pay fewer taxes and to plunder the debts of the state?

Q. The question is wholly legitimate: how would you answer it?

A. From the 1980s onward, capital accumulation has cast off the fet-
ters of democracy and of the philosophy of full employment. A New
Right has taken shape, one that advocates the abolition of all rules respecting the financial markets, of controls over environmental degra-
dation and over workplace conditions, the weakening of the unions and
shifting them from national contracts to ones specific to a particular
enterprise. This phase, the consequences of which Europe has been de-
bating since at least 2011, delineates a mutation in the social conditions
prevailing in democracy.

Q. In your opinion, in what direction is the mutation headed?

A. In the Keynesian past, the breach of the compromise, and the determination to curtail welfare policies, had sometimes involved violent
strategies: as we noted above, the Chilean coup d'état of 1973 saw the
imposition of a free-market turn. Hypothesizing a rerun of that violent

and antidemocratic scenario seems absurd, even if history teaches us to never say never. Another change, perhaps less tragic though not without less suffering, is the one outlined in the last few years through the de-politicization of economic relations and the consolidation of economic inequalities. When accepting the compromise with industrial capital-ism, democracy had claimed that all social relations were political in nature: the intervention of politics in the sphere of the economy was an accepted fact, and civil rights sufficed to limit the decision-making power of the majorities. In this way, democratic politics entered into every crease of society whenever it was a question of reestablishing and defending the equal liberty of citizens that the constitutions en-visaged. When that compromise started collapsing at the end of the 1970s, politics gradually regressed and above all took gigantic strides backward so far as the world of work and industrial relations was con-cerned. Work—we hear more and more often—should return to being an exclusively economic good, one entirely subjected to the market and unhampered by regulation and politics. To a degree, European socie-ties are coming to resemble American society as the ideology preach-ing the necessity of deinstitutionalizing the welfare state has expanded enough to become an accepted given by both the Right and the Left. Today, both center-right and center-left governments pursue the same politics of shrinking state spending on social policies, privatizing social services (also schooling) and thus ascribing responsibility for the crisis to taxation and redistribution. In sum, it seems that the responsibility for the crisis lies with democracy or with the promise it makes of po-litical equality and some basic social conditions of citizenship. This is a disquieting thought.

Q. *You hold that the political battle in Italy over Article 18 of the Workers' Statute has precisely this meaning?*

A. The Workers' Statute (a sort of constitutionalization of labor re-lations) was approved by the Italian Parliament in 1970. Article 18 of this statute regulates and limits the liberty of the employer to fire an employee (this article holds only for medium-large factories or firms) by subjecting the decision to dismiss to a "just cause"; that is, the judge or a tribunal is to give a ruling in cases of contested dismissal. The idea of "just cause" (*giusta causa*) is consistent with Article 41 of the Italian constitution, which declares that private economic activity has social responsibility: "Private-sector economic initiative is freely exercised. It cannot be conducted in conflict with social usefulness or in such a manner that could damage safety, liberty, and human dignity. The law shall provide for appropriate programs and controls so that public and private-sector economic activity may be oriented and coordinated for social purposes."

This means that the Italian constitution does not simply protect the individual right to industrial property: it protects it in exchange for some self-limitation on the part of the employer, who does not make decisions only in order to increase his profit with no regard for their social impact. Social responsibility of capitalist property: this is the meaning of Article 41 of the Italian constitution and Article 18 of the Workers' Charter.

In recent years, several governments have tried to curtail the power of Article 18 and finally to abolish it. It is very telling that the abolition of the Workers' Charter (and Article 18 in particular) was obtained by the center-left government led by Matteo Renzi, who is also the secretary general of the Democratic Party. In opposing the abolition of this article, the representatives of the trades unions have argued that Article 18 has in fact had a very limited impact since it affects only medium and large businesses, whereas the Italian economy is for the most part based upon medium and small or family businesses. The answer to this objection has been that the markets and the investors wanted this change. In other words, it was a decision with a symbolic value. But why did the markets need this kind of signal? The answer may be deduced from what we have said above: the leading force of the new or neoliberal democracy is no longer supposed to be the law (the legislator or the state) but rather the market: thus the idea that a significant portion of the social sphere must revert to being subjected to private interests and therefore exclude interference on the part of politics. The limit of a "just cause" imposed by Article 18 sanctioned the priority of the public over the private in social relationships between people with unequal power: the giver of work was obliged to account for any dismissal and prove the latter to have been dictated only by economic reason and not by discrimination against the fired workers on grounds of ideology, religious belief, gender, etc. The article was in perfect agreement with the philosophy of compromise between democracy and capitalism that oriented social-democratic ideology in postwar Europe: it established for everyone the freedom from domination and from being subjected to the decisions of others for no other reason than the arbitrary will of the one who decides. As noted above, Article 18 was the natural consequence of Article 41 of the Italian constitution, since it imposed civic responsibility upon the sphere of economic interests.

In assessing this new phase of political relations between classes, we need to ask ourselves: what sort of society will it be if accumulation is unhampered by social ties and the political limits to redistribution? Or by any other consideration regarding employment save profit? Or by any responsibility toward the environment and the health of those who work and consume? Are we sure we want to live in a society of this kind?

Q. I would put these selfsame questions to you, and would further add: how much inequality can a democracy bear?

A. Impoverishment and the concentration of wealth go together: this is the law of oligarchy. If the interests of the "few" and the "many" diverge dramatically, we can predict that their interest in cooperating or in seeking compromises or mediation will also decline. The few and the many revert to being two separate societies. Those who have so very much think that they can impose their own choices, relying upon the needs of those who have much less or little. Those who have less or no bargaining power, aside from the political power they have as citizens, know that they have nothing to gain by compromise and that it is in fact to their disadvantage since they have no bargaining power. And the very rich have no interest in submitting to the legal obligation that social democracy imposed on them. The conditions for cooperation between classes diminish, allowing us to glimpse a phenomenon that cannot help but cause concern, namely, class secession from the general interest or political citizenship.

Democracy aspires to be a balance between the classes, in particular between these two opposite sides of the population, which are not monoliths but internally faceted groups. Up until now the democratic compromise has been envisaged, especially by those who were socially weaker, as the main highway to emancipation within the framework of basic individual rights. Democracy arose as a demand for liberty on the part of those who were not powerful enough to obtain freedom by drawing upon their own social or cultural resources. The success of this inclusive politics has been proved by the expansion of the middle class, that is, by the overcoming of a drastic dualism between the few-rich and the many-poor through the formation of a large middle. The expansion of the middle class has corresponded to the expansion of democracy, the victory of democracy over dictatorial regimes after World War II; its restriction (and the exacerbation of the few/many dualism) should set alarm bells ringing.

However, I want to come back to one point: the aim of democracy is the equal opportunity to participate in political choices, which is actually its precondition: the goal of democracy is liberty from domination. For those who do not have social or economic power, the sole resource of liberty as nondomination is represented by the quest for, and the attainment of, political power as equal citizens. Appealing to number and therefore to the capacity to bargain, the many have obtained normative equality with the few and a bargaining power they would not otherwise have. Herein lies the great lesson of democracy: use the instrument of artificial equality in order to be free.

Q. History reminds us that the aristocrats, the powerful, and those you call oligarchs have always felt themselves to be "equal" and deserving of power. Isn't that how it is?

A. They have always been free because they have been socially equal. The strategy of the others, that is, of the majority of the population, of those who do not have the economic means to support themselves autonomously, is laying claim to political power. To obtain it, as we saw in the previous chapter, they fashioned a new type of equality: *isonomia*, that is, equality before the law and in the political power to participate in making decisions on issues pertaining to all or to the general society, to which was added *isegoria*, freedom of speech and active participation in decision making and in the shaping of political opinion. Those who were not equal in material resources made themselves equal through norms and political power, through the instrument of the law, and in this way they became free.

But if the social distance between the few and the many becomes huge, it may happen that the space for compromise shrinks. Whereas in the phase of social democracy both classes felt themselves to be in the same boat, so to speak, and were obliged to arrive at an agreement in the interests of all, in the new free-market phase the few may find it convenient to withdraw and separate themselves from the "wider" society. Since their power to impose their will on the weaker is unparalleled, why should they agree to sacrifice or contain their decision-making power within the domain of economic accumulation and profit? Why not blaze a trail to political power? In essence, financial revenues project them into a global world located outside of state jurisdictions. The very few rich can *secede* from society (and from its costs) and "make a society" on their own account: the transformation of capitalism risks facilitating this trajectory.

By contrast with industrial capital, which is rooted in a territory, financial capital is free from geopolitical and even "ethical" ties. The 1 percent identified by Occupy Wall Street can live where they please, from Paris to New York, London to Singapore, sharing virtually nothing with the many save the vexation of being challenged from time to time. If the oligarchs can live in a cosmopolitan dimension, the same is not true of the many, who have a real need of the state. The few can withdraw and stop paying for the social issues of the many, leaving the latter to worry about their plight and their increasingly unsatisfied needs. Is it perhaps not true that taxes are essentially paid by the many? The ideology of the nation-state is already obsolete for those with the "power to secede." The few pay a risible amount of tax compared to that shelled out by the many. The few pay for the services that serve them (police and army, which protect basic property rights in the domestic sphere and guard against the risk of war); the poor and the middle classes pay, in addition, for other services they cannot by their own means enjoy otherwise (health, schooling, unemployment benefits, etc.). The two groups contribute in relation to what they need: this is a change in the meaning of democracy and the welfare state (no longer universal but tied to needs) that has emerged in Europe in the 1980s, and it is already an indication of secession from responsibility for the public good. The democratic state thus ends up, in advanced societies, by more closely resembling a bargaining confederation of two classes than a state of individuals-citizens.

The theme of the *two societies* reflects the erosion and violation of the compromise. When Western capitalism no longer has to settle accounts with the organized workforce, since its origin has changed, when it in essence depends upon the money invested in the financial markets, and much less in industry, and when it loses visibility as a class and geographical location, then it can probably permit itself the luxury of breaking off relations with a class of people that disturbs, that asks for things, that has needs. If in the past national capitalists had names and physical visibility (identified with a family, for instance), today it is a JSC, a joint-stock company, an acronym on the stock market, a holding, a corporate enterprise behind which there are persons no one knows. We too perhaps are in that JSC, having a limited share through our pension fund, and thus we ourselves are accessories, though unwilling ones, to the mutation.

Q. You referred earlier to the relations between liberty and equality, the subject of your book The Tyranny of the Moderns, *published by Yale University Press.*

A. It seems to me that the implications of that relationship are twofold. First of all, those who question the value of democracy are presumably also convinced that not all persons are deserving of respect because not all are equal. Second, both liberty and equality are artificial creations: they do not occur in nature, although the religious and philosophical arguments regarding human rights have done important ideological work in entrenching the idea that rights are natural. This artificiality means that both these values and democracy are gains that are never guaranteed. Nor are they impervious to risk. It reinforces the conviction that a permanent ideological or educative endeavor to sustain democratic institutions from within is opportune. How? And who should be the protagonists of this education? These questions lead us to distinguish between democracy and other conceptions of free government, for example, republicanism and liberalism. Unlike republicanism, democracy is particularly attentive to political equality and thus does not regard virtue as the engine of civic life, nor does it make citizenship inclusion or recognition conditional upon the acquisition of certain virtues or capacities. In democracy, educative or civic action is *indirect*: it is an unpremeditated achievement through the ordinary working of political procedures and institutions and through the practice of respect that, by virtue of rights and wise rules, establishes interpersonal relationships consistent with these principles. Once subjects become citizens, political and legal institutions start to have some influence on people's mentality and behavior and also on their passions and interests. Yet they are included *before* this happens, not *on condition* that this happen: to become democratic citizens we are not required to prove that we are virtuous or can reason correctly. Unlike liberalism, on the other hand, democracy assigns a central role to political inclusion and participation, whether in the guise of the decision-making process, such as the vote, or in that of the public presence of ideas and the formation and manifestation of opinions, through movements, the press, and political parties.

Q. *This is not to claim, however, that capitalism only arises in a democracy, given not only the case of contemporary China but also that of many nations in Southeast Asia, let alone the extreme case of Pinochet's Chile.*

A. This realization is of great significance and altogether new. Indeed, during the Cold War—when on the one hand there were countries that were neither democratic nor free market, beginning with the Soviet Union, and on the other hand the democratic and free-market nations—the two factors were thought to be correlated, or at any rate it was supposed that they could advance together. One might say that a limited territory was an obstacle that hindered the capacity of capitalism to express all its potentially destructive force. The end of "realized" socialism has highlighted the possibility of a "real" capitalism, that is to say, capitalism without democracy, and the economic crisis in societies with established democracies is provoking in its turn a short circuit in the relationships between these two systems. A democratic government needs a space that has limits, but capitalism tends to overcome all spatial limitation so as to reach all countries and markets. This is an additional factor that proves that, once the Cold War was over, the compromise between democracy and capitalism started becoming difficult to maintain and in fact was anachronistic.

So long as capitalist accumulation was directed at the production and distribution of consumer goods within a market not yet wholly globalized, for instance within a national society, thereby generating a sustained demand for labor power within a delimited territory and a controlled number of people (workforce), the capitalism-democracy agreement worked. For broad swathes of the population, it created living conditions wholly unprecedented in the history of the West and an expansion in individual life opportunities. But the crisis erupting in 2008, which has been no less epoch making than the one at the end of the 1920s (which, it is worth recalling, brought low several liberal and constitutional states), has revealed a crack in this alliance.

Capital is directed toward production in those areas of the world in which production can make a stratospheric profit due precisely to the absence of human rights and civil and political rights. Capitalism profits much more when and if people are subjected to political systems that do not entrench their decisions within procedures based on equal political rights and some civil rights. Moreover, it is directed toward the maximization and monopolistic accumulation of financial profit, with the result that the development of capitalism is on a collision course with democracy, favoring—as Habermas has argued—a depoliticization of some important spheres of social life, so as to prevent the democratic legislator from being able to interfere and make decisions that impose limits and threaten the interests of the oligarchies. Faced with a picture of this kind, we are tempted to ask whether Marx was perhaps not right.

Q. And how do you answer? Was Marx right?

A. Sometimes I tend to think that he was. With his corrosive realism and his unrivaled rhetorical style, he had responded with a measure of sarcasm to democratic ideology's ambition to create an abstract political sphere and legal equality in order to render everyone free within the public domain, although not in social and economic power (and therefore in actual fact not autonomous so far as freedom of choice was concerned). As we know, for Marx such a compromise between classes so unequal in social power was not possible (and indeed a mockery); for the social democrats it was possible. However, we should not linger over Marx's skepticism but rather reflect upon the erosion of the compromise between labor and capital, democracy and capitalism. During World War II, democracy appealed to the pragmatic optimism of the social democrats, who sought to demonstrate, against the free marketeers and against Marx, that it was possible to keep political separate from economic power without jeopardizing economic freedom or inhibiting accumulation. Our democracies were born out of a balance between social classes. They are the daughters of the social-democratic strategies conceived in the aftermath of the crisis of 1929 (the repression of political liberty) and designed to neutralize any possibility of a relapse. They have been democracies based upon full employment or upon a political equality sustained by the promise of full employment. Postwar reconstruction may well have lent credence to this optimism because the sheer scale of the destruction required literally the full employment of all citizens in the reconstruction. This compromise has come to an end, or at any rate it has very plainly cracked. All that the Western democracies have built up as a public good (education, healthcare, and provision for the elderly), paid for through an active politics promoting employment, has entered into crisis.

Q. *Equality—you have said—is a principle of relationship and not one of substance. If that is so, why do you think that the privatization of goods such as education or health is a problem for democracy rather than a resource?*

A. It bears repeating: political equality is normative in nature, not sociological; it has to do with public relationships between citizens, not the equalization of their social or specific identities. Democracy does not say that all are equal because all are identical. Quite the reverse. It in fact asserts that we must be treated as equal precisely because equal we are not, either in ideas, in economic circumstances, or in gender and culture. As we said in the previous chapter, it endeavors to block the translation of differences into inequalities of political power because the latter can give rise to domination. If it endeavors to be more than this, equality risks becoming very problematic for liberty: this is why we should not stray beyond the bounds of the concept of relationship.

Q. *Let us return to speaking of the goods that democracy should keep well away from the market and not privatize, because upon this, as you have just said, a crucial fact depends: equality as a condition of political liberty. What part does education have to play in the mutation of democracy?*

A. Let us get down to brass tacks and return to the argument about the role of public education and schools mentioned at the start of our conversation. You will remember that we promised to return to it. I would like to use Italy as a test case to prove that public goods are under threat of being privatized and that this compromises gravely the functioning and quality of democracy. Italy is an interesting case because it built a solid public system of education from the time of its unification, when only a privileged few could profit by it: those who enjoyed the right to vote. In Italy, the trajectory of political emancipation (from limited to universal suffrage) went along with the expansion of other basic goods, like education. Hence, the constitution of the Italian Republic, which became operational on January 1, 1949, contains some important articles concerning the enjoyment of specific public goods, among them primary education. Article 33 thus states very clearly that primary education is free but that it does not rely upon public funding: "The Republic guarantees the freedom of the arts and sciences, which may be freely taught. The Republic lays down general rules for education and establishes state schools for all branches and grades. Entities and private persons have the right to establish schools and institutions of education at no cost to the State." This article does not stand alone, at odds with the other principles affirmed in the constitution. It states that private institutions are free to establish schools but with no burden on the state. They can ask for and obtain, under the appropriate circumstances that ordinary law defines, recognition from the republic: "The law, when setting out the rights and obligations for nonstate schools which request parity shall ensure that these schools enjoy full liberty and offer their pupils an education and qualifications of the same standards as those afforded to pupils in state school." Yet even in the case in which nonstate schools have been granted "parity" with state schools they cannot receive state money.

Q. Why is the Italian constitution so concerned not to fund nonstate schools?

A. First of all, to guarantee that the public does not sponsor religious or other identitary kinds of education, and consequently to give all the chance to acquire an education. Public schools are also feeless schools—this is a crucial condition for making possible a truly equal opportunity as regards access to education. Thus there are two reasons for Article 33: equality of opportunity and liberty from nonpublic reasons for exclusion or discrimination. We should not forget that Italy is a predominantly Catholic country. Indeed, we could say that it is a monoreligious democracy, which Article 7 of the Italian constitution recognizes, endorsing the 1929 Concordat between the government (then headed by Mussolini) and the Vatican, thus agreeing to make the Catholic Church a privileged interlocutor of the Italian state. The revision of the Concordat in 1984 has ended this situation of *cuius regio eius religio* (each state with its own official religion)—without, however, annulling it. Indeed, Article 33 anticipated somehow that religious schools would try to extend their influence in society and to diminish the role of state schools. But Article 33 implies more than that, as I have mentioned above. It implies and indeed states that education is a good open to all children and that it should not aim at forming religious citizens but rather citizens who are free to have a religious faith. Article 33 is a proclamation of equality and openness. In Italy, then, public schooling does not answer only to a demand for equal opportunities as the material conditions that give free and universal access to a good education. It answers also to a demand for pluralism and laicity, which means equality of consideration before and by the law. On the one hand, Article 33 sanctions the existence of public education, to which all contribute financially because it does not bear the hallmark of any religious or ideological credo; on the other hand, it is concerned to ensure that education is not confessional, precisely in order to render it inclusive and open to all, without identitarian specifications, be they secularist in kind or religious.

Article 33 is a promise of *laicité*, a word the English language renders, unfortunately, as secularism. Yet *laicité* is not an ideology since it does not declare that the school should promote a statist vision or an antireligious perspective. It is instead an attitude of the civil authority toward religious practices with the aim of rendering them capable of living peacefully together with nonreligious practices or the practices of other religions. *Laicité* is a way of achieving the coexistence of diverse creeds in a climate of freedom so that each person can choose whether to believe and which religion to join. It means, in a word, the generality of the civil law. Freedom of conscience is the core of *laicité* (and Article 33). The goal of *laicité* is to ensure first of all civil peace (for society) and security (for the individual), or the certainty that differences (of faith or ideology or culture) are not a cause of intolerance, discrimination, and violence. To obtain this, the civil authority has to make laws and apply them in such a way that they are and remain as much as possible free from specific doctrinal contents (even if and when these contents are shared by a large majority of the population). The *laicité* of a law is the measure of its generality, the index of its capacity to include all citizens equally, not only those who are aligned with the faith or view shared by the majority. As we said in a previous chapter, right does its job of protecting the individual from state power or the power of persons provided it is not owned by the majority, or a portion, of the population. Thus, *laicité* is the same thing as the *generality of the law*, and it is the condition of pluralism. This makes it also the condition of civil peace because from respect for pluralism of opinions and of associations there stems security for individuals along with an open society. Liberty and peace are neatly connected to the *laicité* of the civil law as a project of protection for the equal treatment of all citizens. The equality provision is a predicate of liberty.

In a monoreligious country like Italy, post-1945 members of the Constituent Assembly decided that a public system of education would exist, serving as a home for all children in which they would relate to their peers from families with different beliefs, classes, and ideological convictions. Article 33 says in sum that children are not the property of their parents but are persons who are potentially autonomous and thus in need of education to achieve their full independence from tutelage. Most of the time, when parents claim a religiously based education for their children in the name of their freedom of education, they are actually claiming a sort of property right over their children, extending to them their own faith as if their liberty coincided with their children's liberty.

The public school, as Piero Calamandrei (one of the most prominent Italian jurists of the twentieth century and a member of the Constitutional Assembly) wrote on several occasions, is the basic condition for a pluralistic society that is respectful of individuals' differences without being indifferent or dismissive. This is the political philosophy buttressing Article 33. In today's Italy, this article is under threat and although never formally modified is under a process of ideological revision because de facto many Catholic schools receive funds from local governments. The undeclared goal of this revision is that of allowing private (but in fact Catholic) schools to have free access to public money. The practical possibility for that project came to be realized with the process of federalization of the Italian state, which started in the 1990s and opened the door to the decentralization of primary public school administration. Under the pressure of local communities' requests to have a say in the administration of schools, and moreover under the pressure of the financial crisis, which translated into devastating cuts in public spending, local governments (the municipalities) reinterpreted de facto the concept of "the public" so as to make it inclusive of the "whole" system of education, thus of state schools and nonstate "parified" schools (that is, nonstate schools that have been granted "parity" with state schools as regards the qualifications they award their students).

Q. A very fierce debate is currently underway concerning the public funding of private schools, a debate that goes beyond any question of efficiency or the allocation of resources, promoting instead opposing visions of the role of education in a democracy.

A. I want first of all to raise and discuss the *subsidiarity* argument that has been used to defend state funding of private schools. As the former MP Giancarla Codrignani has explained very clearly in commenting on the new law that opened the doors to the public funding of religious schools, what served as the pacesetter in the education debate was an "intriguing" word recently inserted into the newly written section of the Italian constitution known as "Titolo V" (Section or Title V), which regulates the powers and prerogatives of the regions, provinces, and municipalities. This new part of the Italian constitution was passed in 2001, under pressure from the Northern League to transform the Italian republic into a federation. Title V does not in fact institute a federal state; it does, however, introduce a remarkable degree of regional autonomy so far as taxation and the management of public services like health and education are concerned. Under this new constitutional law, compulsory school (from nursery school at the age of five to the eighth grade) was made the responsibility of local government. Here is what Article 118 (Article 24 of Title V) says: "Administrative functions are attributed to the Municipalities, unless they are attributed to the Provinces, Metropolitan Cities and Regions or to the State, pursuant to the principles of subsidiarity, differentiation, and proportionality, to ensure their uniform implementation."

In an article for the newspaper *La Repubblica* Codrignani has written that in 2001, the year the reform of the constitution passed, "subsidiarity" was a very problematic term, politically and juridically, because of its vagueness and its polemical connotations (the term "subsidiarity" was used by its proponents as an expression of antistate regionalism). And there was no shortage of warnings:

> Given the lack of clear juridical definitions, subsidiarity can mean that the private sector does what the state—human needs being virtually unlimited—does not manage to do, or that the state limits itself to what private organizations do not manage to do. Even then a part of the Left (the part that despaired of ever reforming the welfare state and capitulated before the doctrine of market-inspired policies or services no longer controlled by the state), was prefiguring the second possibility [that the state limits itself to what private organizations do not manage to do]. What a pity that it persisted with empty talk about reformism, without acknowledging that the transformation of the traditional welfare state into a politics of succor for the needy (managed by private and religious organizations most of the time) was already underway.

This quotation contains the gist of my argument. It is also worth bringing to the fore the bipartisan aspect, because the mutations, when they are so radical, transcend party positions and ideological differences; they become, as I noted when answering your first question, molecular transformations of the whole society. "Subsidiarity" is the ideology that, after the demise of traditional political ideologies, has dominated the political arena in Italy since the 1990s, paving the way for the doctrinaire justification of the interchangeability of the public and the private. This same criterion inspired Title V of the Italian constitution: a reform that has led to deterioration in the quality of the public function in our country, boosting the power of local authorities but without subjecting it to an equally strong supervisory power over the use of resources.

Q. *Let us linger over the campaign for so-called educational freedom, which, as you pointed out at the start of our conversation and as you have repeated here, has assumed a symbolic value in the great mutation now under way.*

A. The campaign began after the system of corruption exploded ("Tangentopoli"—or "Bribesville," as it was called—started in 1992). It was accompanied by the collapse and in some cases disappearance of the old parties that had governed in postwar Italy and the sudden change of political personnel caused by the criminal responsibility of the old political elite. The change was so radical that commentators and politicians started talking of a "Second Republic"—although it would perhaps be more appropriate to call it the "lesser republic" since in truth it was not a regime change but a change (somehow for the worse) of political personnel at the top and intermediate levels. Political support for that constitutional reform was almost unanimous and cut across conventional ideological lines. At the same time Italy witnessed a renewed activism of religion in the public sphere, serving to jeopardize, rather than safeguard, the premises of respect for pluralism. It seems to me of interest to discuss it precisely in terms of the philosophy of freedom of educational supply with which the campaign has defended the public support (that is, in the guise of public money) granted to private schools ever since it first appeared, fifteen years ago, and which has led to the Berlinguer reform, named after the minister of education Luigi Berlinguer, who launched it during the center-left governments led by Romano Prodi and Massimo D'Alema in 1999 and 2000.

Q. *The idea of the public funding of private schools began with the hypothesis of providing families with* buoni-scuola *(school vouchers), the state not being able to fund private schools directly, given what is laid down in Article 33 of the Italian constitution.*

A. At the time at which the question was first broached, perhaps shortly after 1996, Dario Antiseri, one of the most effective and combative free-market theorists, defended the school vouchers, harping on the theme of freedom of choice, or again on feelings of altruism and generosity toward the poor. Apart from that—and this was Antiseri's second point—just as only the better-off have sufficient means to enroll their children in private schools, the state needs to offer this same choice to whosoever desires it, in order that there not be discrimination for economic reasons. To rectify what free marketeers and Catholics call "the absence of educational freedom for families," the state should distribute school vouchers in order to render all citizens equal.

Q. *The law of 2000 on educational parity seems to have implemented this philosophy.*

A. At first glance the argument regarding freedom of choice seems well put. But it is an abstract argument that, moreover, espouses the idea that the state should not simply defend freedom of educational choice but should also support the choice of parents to send their children to religious or private schools with its own money, and this is truly questionable. The state assuredly should not obstruct freedom of choice (hence Article 33 declares that private schools are free), yet is it reasonable for it to give individuals money (vouchers) with the goal of making their freedom actual? The state gives citizens free schooling: this is the free choice that it guarantees. Yet if some parents want to renounce sending their children to the feeless schools offered by the state and prefer private schools (for reasons of their own), then this cannot be a justification for asking for a voucher or, as is now the case, for tax exemption on the fee paid to a private school. Although the logic informing this argument is neoliberal and antistate, it speaks for a highly interventionist state that actually promotes private schooling and makes its own schools weaker by taking away from them money in order to subsidize a family's choice to spend money on a private (and generally inferior) school. Moreover, this spuriously neoliberal argument is abstract because it does not take into account the concrete circumstances prevailing in Italy (namely, its monoreligious character, as noted above), which gives a political advantage to one religious group. Thus in Italy, the free-choice argument voiced by the free marketeers translates into its opposite. Up until today, in the great majority of cases, parents have no reasonable interest in enrolling their children in private schools, since they are generally worse than the public ones. What then is the use of vouchers or financial support to families enabling their children to choose private schools during the years of compulsory education? Two considerations come to mind: in the first place, as was said, one does not fund the freedom to choose with public money. The state should remove obstacles of a legal kind, for example by according parity to the examination certificates issued by the private schools (after of course having validated them) and therefore by not disincentivizing choice. But the state cannot fund free choice. In the second place, if the aim is not to correct a situation of inequality or of qualitative scarcity, since the private schools do not offer better services, why should the state ever facilitate choice in the private sector? The suspicion arises that the intervention in support of private schools will end up by bringing about a situation of inequality where there was not one before, artificially producing a market in education. In short, private supply is created with public money.

Q. *What is your fundamental objection?*

A. The argument of the free marketeers, which may seem logical in theory, is in contradiction with the Italian situation because in Italy the private schools account for 5–7 percent of the supply of education, and, moreover, they are not as good as public schools. What then would be the aim of introducing the funding of private schools through a voucher system? As I see it, the free marketeers want to use public money to create artificially a market that does not exist. They use this expedient like the government incentive for the scrapping of old automobiles: with the difference—and for the worse—that the car industry was an undoubtedly significant reality (although those incentives have not served to save it from an inexorable decline) while private schooling is not a significant reality at all. One can have no objection to private persons or groups who seek to invest in education: entrepreneurial freedom exists, and Article 33 of the Italian constitution recognizes it. What should arouse suspicion, however, is the "statism of the free marketeers," in other words, the fact of their wishing to create a market with taxpayer money. This insidious strategy is meant to privatize the entire system of education, that is to say, to create or expand inequality.

Q. *Bill Clinton, the former U.S. president, made school vouchers one of the lynchpins of his electoral campaign, and all in the name of equality of opportunity and therefore of equal liberty.*

A. Bill Clinton may well have had sound reasons for proposing vouchers. In the United States, in fact, public schools have been deteriorating for some time. Being funded through local property taxes, they are directly linked to the social conditions in the neighborhoods in which they are built. In the poorer urban areas, therefore, the schools are very bad and attended mostly by the poor. Class structure is the problem here. The "secession" of the better-off from the inner city to the suburbs served to impoverish public education in the urban areas, to the detriment of those who are not rich enough to enroll their children in private schools or to move. The vouchers were designed to remedy that situation of injustice and lack of liberty. Except that, after years of experimentation, the outcome of this policy turned out to be a disaster: first of all, because it impoverished still more the public schools, given that, to fund the vouchers, the money was diverted from the public toward the private schools. The vouchers were in fact used by students from the middle class to "migrate" from the public schools, which were often not good, to a private school or to a public school that was better but located in another quarter, one not inhabited by poor people. The situation worsened so dramatically that when in 2000 Al Gore ran for the White House, he changed strategy, no longer relying on the vouchers but on directly funding the public schools in order to improve them.

Q. Aside from these empirical considerations regarding the impact of the vouchers, are there any other objections?

A. Yes. They have to do with the principles of liberty and tolerance. As a 2001 ruling by the Florida Supreme Court has shown, funding private schools (and therefore also religious ones) with public money is in conflict with the First Amendment, what in America is called the rule of the "wall," that is, the principle of separation between state and church, which serves to safeguard religious pluralism and is therefore another important liberty.

In Italy, the republican state was not inspired by the philosophy of the "wall" but instead adopted a concordatory policy. Nonetheless, while conceding a prominent role to the Church of Rome, the Italian constitution has undertaken not to allocate public funds to private schools (which are mostly Catholic), and therefore not even to religious ones, not only so as not to impoverish the public but also out of respect for the principles of religious pluralism and of equality. In the case of education, we encounter the same idiom of the wall between public and private.

Q. The widening of the socioeconomic gap is leading to a generalized call for greater equity: in recent years, the theme has featured again and again in the speeches of many world leaders, from Barack Obama to Pope Francis. How should we define equity? And is it perhaps an antidote to the risks of democratic regression?

A. In the current situation, the relationship between equality and equity becomes crucial. Equity is a virtue of distributive justice. It implies that, if in the distribution of certain goods the criterion of equality of treatment should apply, the public (that is, those who are distributing) should pay particular attention to the specific conditions in which the recipients of the distribution happen to find themselves. In contrast to simple or horizontal equality, the norm of equal treatment requires that these specificities be known and considered in such a way that contrary effects are not produced. But, as a "virtue," equity is not measurable with mathematical precision. Even if the parameters for the measurement of needs, possibilities, and objectives are defined in advance, decisions that are not strictly functional or "just" are liable to be made. Public policies take for granted the limits of abstraction characteristic of statistical measurements, and it is up to the prudence of the actor (the judge or civil servant) to maintain a certain elasticity in their decision making. This is why, when we move from general criteria to practical implementation, in justice as in equity we may encounter decisions that are mistaken and less than just toward every individual.

Going back to the question: no, equity is not in itself an antidote to democratic regression. Furthermore, it presupposes concord between the classes: that is to say, it assumes that social inequalities have no power over the law and that the degree of partisan discretionality remains low. Concord between the classes can more readily be translated as equal consideration. But if the few no longer wish to share the same fate as the many and therefore refuse to submit to the same rules and the same distributive criteria, equity too becomes a sorry thing: a fig leaf that scarcely covers materiality.

Q. One of the recurrent fears that emanates from our dialogue is of democracy growing progressively more weary. Do you reckon that the antiegalitarian mutation is a litmus test of this phenomenon?

A. We have just said that legal equality as a principle held the promise of being an artificial strategy serving to minimize the risks of discrimination that social differences and inequalities can facilitate. But when the state lowers its guard, the sociological specificities tend to become stronger and to be transferred into the political sphere, laying claim to a greater measure of recognition. In *The Future of Democratic Equality*, Joseph M. Schwartz blames these dynamics upon the identitary politics pursued over the last few decades. Ethnic, geographical, or religious identity has become so strong—this is Schwartz's argument—as to all but represent a criterion for the selective distribution of goods that should instead be equally shared among everyone. The citizen seems almost to disappear behind his or her preponderant form of belonging. Those concerned to monitor the antiegalitarian mutation would do well to pay particular attention to the administering of justice. Liberal thinkers have considered it to be essential to any understanding of the dynamics of society. Justice is costly, and in every Western society we are witness to the fact that those without economic resources enjoy worse services. It is true that those who need a lawyer and lack the wherewithal to pay for one can avail themselves of legal aid, yet we know that it is a service of inferior quality to private legal advice (this basic right is being eroded in many established democracies, to the point that Stephen Holmes has observed that the "rule of law" and equal treatment under the law are more a privilege for those who can afford a legal service than a right). And inequalities appear in all their gravity in the weaker segments of the population. John Rawls argued that justice should neutralize two great factors of inequality in the distribution of opportunities: fortune and nature. No one should pay for what they are not responsible for: either because they came into the world with disabilities or because they were born into a family of ne'er-do-wells. The democracies—these artificial systems of norms that, remarkably, render equal in something so relevant as political power those who are not equal—were also born with the promise of justice: a promise that has not been kept and one that now is actually considered by many to be a promise that is exaggerated or even not to be honored.

Q. *Can you give us some examples?*

A. In Italy, the mutation we are discussing consists in restricting the opportunities open to young people by treating them de facto differently or according to the region, the class, the family, and even the neighborhood they come from. These social backgrounds are much more important in determining individuals' futures now than they were in past decades, when the equalizing function of social policies and public schooling was still working well. Up until the 1970s and mid-1980s, those in Italy who came from working-class families had more possibilities of gaining access to a good public school and then to a good university education, and therefore to improving their own chances as far as work and career were concerned. Elsa Fornero, appointed minister of labor in 2011 in the Monti administration, said in an interview that thanks to her education at a public school she had managed to become a university professor. Her personal abilities had come to the fore, and her ambitions had not been thwarted by her social origins.

Giving everyone a chance to recognize their own vocation and to commit themselves to realizing it is one of the challenges of justice and democracy. One of the primary aims of a public system of education should be that of allowing each young person to understand what they wish to do in life and develop their capacities in order to attain that objective. The equal chance to develop one's capabilities does not mean that there is a right to become an Albert Einstein, but it does mean to so arrange things that, whoever so wishes, should have the chance to develop that potential and those capacities that enable them to become an accomplished mathematician, and not be penalized for reasons that have nothing to do with their will and their intelligence or indeed with their family of origin, their gender, or their coming from one part of the country rather than another.

The individual person is therefore integral to the preoccupations of democracy. But the mutation now underway increases the importance of groups, corporations, and class identities, rendering the future of each less open to the direct involvement of individuals. We seem to see once again in operation the logic of the society of the ancien régime, where castes decided the fate of persons and where individual commitment was a secondary or accidental factor in the race of life.

Q. *Equality makes it possible to establish meritocratic principles in society as opposed to privilege.*

A. Whenever the principle of equality is violated, merit, that is, individual commitment, is betrayed: this does not gainsay the fact that in situations of exceptional seriousness—and this is entirely legitimate—policies have been devised that do not treat everyone equally and that take discriminatory factors into account, supporting and assisting those who otherwise would have no chance of fully expressing their own potential or of competing on a level playing field.

In the United States policies involving affirmative action (or, in other words, promoting equal opportunities) represented active intervention on the part of the law to block the impact of racial or gender factors upon the job market or access to education. A society implementing such policies is openly admitting itself to be unjust and to have no other path to follow in the short term but that of making choices that, in strict principle, are unjust because they are not impartial toward sociocultural differences and involve a reverse discrimination serving to remedy the effects occasioned by a secular injustice suffered by certain minorities.

These are, however, public decisions based upon a principle: the distribution of goods and sacrifices should follow the criterion of equal treatment, and this, under conditions of major economic disequilibrium, can mean taking the specificities of the life conditions of persons into account, in other words, not treating them with blind impartiality or with neutrality. For this reason, an argument about merit detached from a person's social circumstances is abstract and risks being unjust.

Q. But is it really possible to anchor merit to social conditions?

A. In his novel *The House of the Seven Gables*, Nathaniel Hawthorne has the idealist Mr. Holgrave inveigh against the "odious and abominable past" that oppresses individuals "with all its bad influences": "Shall we never, never get rid of this past? . . . It lies upon the present like a giant's dead body . . . ! Whatever we seek to do, of our own free motion, a dead man's icy hand obstructs us!" Hawthorne thought that if "each generation were allowed and expected to build its own houses, that single change, comparatively unimportant in itself, would imply almost every reform which society is now suffering for" because it would render each individual truly able to express himself and enable society truly to reward merit. Naturally, this was a provocative response. Nonetheless, its meaning can be decoded as follows: a periodic starting from scratch, every generation, draws attention to the difficulty of making merit the lynchpin of social justice. When one speaks of merit, one should take into account the fact that only a society that accepts a generational resetting of fortune will be able to reward individual merit with justice.

Q. The difficulty of combining society and individuality has been very clearly articulated by the two American philosophers most representative of democratic modernity: John Dewey and John Rawls.

A. In 1916 Dewey wrote that "the accidental qualities of birth, wealth, and knowledge always tend to restrict the opportunities of some as against others." When in *A Theory of Justice* (1971) John Rawls laid down the principles of distributive justice that, in his view, ought to serve to correct the "unequal inheritance of wealth" and remove power "from circumstances, institutions, and historical traditions," he was reviving Hawthorne's theme of the struggle against the past, in other words, against the accumulation of social capital. The task of justice consists, on the one hand, of preventing the "accidents" of first and second nature from weighing upon the distribution of freedoms and opportunities and, on the other hand, of presiding over the threshold of "past time" and defending the prerogatives of the present, in which our choices take place. Democratic political culture, literary and philosophical, both in the past and in recent times, is deeply marked by the awareness that the equal dignity of persons is the fundamental principle in the name of which some inequality of treatment is justified. In the eponymous Platonic dialogue, Protagoras justifies proportional equality in the distribution of recognition as follows: while exclusion from the *demos* fuels the resentment of the excluded, the distribution of public honors in accordance with merit can engender admiration and emulation. Stimulating citizens' faith in their own enterprise, the competition for honors also encourages them to develop their individual potentialities. No one feels outraged, Protagoras says, if a virtuous citizen wins a competition against a citizen who is not virtuous and who is mediocre. For example, in a city of flute players in which everyone is taught to play, citizens would be rebuked or criticized whenever they played badly "instead of being envied for playing well." Envy and offence would arise if other criteria, apart from the ability to play the flute, were used to decide who should play in public. Thus, the unequal distribution of social influence does not humiliate citizens when the system gives everyone the chance to compete on terms of parity and then selects the most deserving. The defense of competition and of merit mounted by Protagoras acquires still more value if compared with the oligarchical criterion. Herodotus recounts how the Spartans and the Egyptians conferred honors and public office on the grounds of family belonging. The son of a flute player was entitled to play the flute, and individual talent was not rewarded: "They play their instrument by right of birth."

Q. *The arguments of Protagoras and Herodotus were reiterated by the last great advocate of the Athenian democracy, Demosthenes.*

A. And closer to our own day, in the mid–nineteenth century, John Stuart Mill wrote that "no one save a mad man would be offended by the fact that there are others whose opinion, and even some whose will, is accorded greater respect than their own." Every individual's present would be able to count as a proof of his merits only if, and for so long as, the "accidents" of birth and social situation (being born into one family rather than another, having one skin color rather than another, being a man rather than a woman, coming from one continent or country rather than another) will not weigh upon the formation of competences and the expression of talents. Justice proposes to correct, contain, or neutralize the role of accident (first nature) and of social determination (second nature) in the distribution of rewards and honors. The utopia of *kallypolis* identified in the *Republic* was founded very perspicaciously upon the neutralization of the role of the family and of property in the appraisal of political competences, because both translated into partiality of judgment and injustice. Placing all children in the ideal circumstance of receiving the same educational grounding and the same stimuli, one can so arrange things that each of them knows their own capacities. By preventing economic circumstances from dictating which persons were to be chosen, one would be able to give everyone the chance to cultivate their own capacities. Plato's logic was not in the least absurd, even though his actual political proposal is unacceptable to anyone who thinks that politics is the locus of liberty.

Q. *How many Italian children wonder each day why the fact of having been born into one social class or in one year rather than in another should determine their place in society?*

A. And then how many of them feel chained to a precarious condition that nothing will ever change, and certainly not their initiative? How many children feel it to be unjust that they are judged not in terms of what they know how to do but in terms of their belonging to a particular family, clan, network, or group? How many of them would wish to be given the chance to be tried and tested by virtue of their own endeavors? How many of them wonder why the fact of having been born in one part of Italy rather than another, although they have attended the same kind of school and pay taxes to the same government, is translated into such different lives and opportunities? How many of them would wish that Whitman's words—"believe in yourself"—were not hollow and utopian?

Q. *These are troubling questions. How do you answer?*

A. The children are right, and the argument about merit cannot disregard these questions. "Meritocracy" has become the magic word brandished by many—on the Left even more than on the Right—because it seems capable of freeing Italian society from its chronic aberrations, its corruption, and its injustice. If merit were really to be recognized, it is said, our society would liberate itself from the snares of nepotism and clientelism, thereby releasing human resources indispensable for the generating of dynamism and justice. As the subtitle of Roger Abravanel's book *Meritocracy* states, this is the recipe for properly valuing talent and rendering "our country richer and more just."

Q. Meritocracy has been defined as a system of government or an organization of collective action based upon "proven ability" and upon "talent" rather than upon "inherited wealth, family and patronage relationships, nepotism, class privilege, property, or other historical factors of political power and social position."

A. Dewey and Rawls would of course have endorsed this definition, but they would have been very skeptical about the idea of meritocracy being a solution to the crux of injustice. Why is it so hard to explain precisely what "real" merit is? First of all because it is impossible to establish with rigor and certainty the correct balance between personal capacities and social circumstances, between "who we are" in the abstract and "who we are in this specific life we are leading": with this bank balance, this identity card, this age, and so on. Sometimes we seem to understand that merit is a quality that a person deemed to be meritorious possesses *naturally*, as through an innate disposition, and that through effort and hard work he brings out. As if a person were from the cradle a good doctor or unemployed, and all that he is or is not, that he has done or has not done, is essentially a personal disposition. We need, however, to pay attention to the social dimension of merit, to its dependence upon social recognition, to the relationship between, for instance, the professions needed in a specific society and the capabilities young people are able to develop so that they can competently function within those professions.

Judgment of a person's merits is relative to a particular sector of work, to determinate requirements that define a performance, to the social usefulness of functions in a given historical period, or to public recognition. Merit involves not only the intrinsic and moral qualities of the person but also what for Adam Smith was the result of a kind of sympathetic correspondence between individual and society. Consequently, modern theorists of justice have always mistrusted this criterion if used to distribute resources. Not because they doubt that you should be a good doctor to be employed by a hospital but because they are wary of mistaking the effect for the cause. Equality of treatment and of opportunity is the principle that should govern justice, not merit: which if anything is a consequence of a just social order. In order not to be fraudulent privilege, merit must emerge from a society in which everyone was granted an equal chance and background to form their own capacities and accede to primary goods, starting with civil rights and the social rights needed to participate in the race of life. In the mid–nineteenth century, Mill proposed that the British Museum be kept open on holidays so that the workers would have the chance to admire beauty and to discover a world of sentiments and pleasures that was denied them. He also thought that those who were not exposed from infancy to cultural stimuli suffered a "loss" that personal initiative could hardly on its own make good, and he concluded by saying that a society that dispenses unequal formative opportunities and stimuli is unjust and should be reformed.

Q. *The idea of justice as distribution of equal formative opportunities has been the backbone of modern democratic thought.*

A. In the mid-1960s, Lyndon B. Johnson, the president of the United States, used to explain how urgent his program for social justice was by telling the following story. Imagine, he said, a race between two persons who set out from the same point, but one of them has laces tied around his ankles that prevent them from being used with their full strength, so that after a few meters he is at an irremediable disadvantage. Can we disregard this difference in capacity when judging the merit of the winner?

Q. *Obviously not.*

A. In this case in fact the winner has no merit, since if anything he enjoys a privilege. For the race to be a genuine contest one would have to remove the obstacles that restrict one of the two competitors *ex ante*. This can be done in three ways: either one frees the person when the race has already begun and pretends that it is a fair contest (but in fact it is simply a matter of privilege), or one gives whoever is faced with an objective obstacle an advantage once the race has begun (that is to say, programs of aid to whoever needs them), or training opportunities are offered to all the competitors before the race begins and with a view to the real race of life (that is to say, policies of social citizenship). These are three different solutions, as may be seen, but they are obscured, or not really brought out, by the vulgate of "meritocracy." President Johnson meant that there cannot be a "merited" merit if some start with an advantage or if the inequalities of opportunity as regards access are not corrected. Which is why, if social relations are not reset, and if society is not refounded from scratch every generation, as the idealist in *The House of the Seven Gables* advocated, we cannot honestly talk of merit as the solution to the problems of injustice. Merit translates as legitimate inequality—more social recognition to some than to others—only if the reasons for the merit are incorporated into a society that has and practices a just politics concerning access to basic resources.

Q. How should one intervene in a society that seeks to turn individual merit into a value to be rewarded?

A. Much has been said about the aberrations that afflict the Italian universities. Faced with the shameful phenomena of corruption our immediate impulse must be to think that the only solution to cure the patient of its corruption is to starve it of resources. To cure a university that does not always select on grounds of merit one must cut its finances, or so it is asserted on all sides and, ever more frequently, by those seeking to further their cause by more or less consciously impoverishing education. In the premodern period, it was thought that the best way to cure a sick person was to bleed them in order to remove the bad blood. Since it was not possible precisely to identify bad blood, one often ended up causing the death of the poor wretch one was actually trying to cure. The body is not reinvigorated by depriving it of food but by giving it good food. This is not necessarily a swift therapy, but it is the only reasonable one. There is no fast justice, despite what the utopians of meritocracy believe. It is not by cutting finances that one can heal the university, not least because the politics of "less cash" does not necessarily translate as "more honesty." It is instead necessary for the money to be better spent and for rigorous systems of selection and supervision to be put in place or implemented, if need be with the application of the penal code and effective systems of recruitment. But we should be under no illusions as to the swiftness of the cure. For it is clear that the question of merit is neither neutral nor a simple matter of procedure. It is also the reflection of an ethical structure shaping social functions, that is to say, a question of who assesses and who is assessed, of systems of assessment, of who devises them and who applies them. It is not enough to articulate the criterion of merit (and which other if not that?); one must actually always follow it. From experience, I must say that often also those who exalt merit are not always ready to honor it, because the logic of the system prevails against honesty and merit.

Q. *Is not this the reason why it is so difficult for an external candidate to win a competitive exam at an Italian university?*

A. If the question of merit has to do with equal opportunities and public ethics, easy solutions are not feasible. Even if one can readily comprehend those who react by wishing to reset everything when faced with some scandal, even if there is nothing new about it, concerning chairs earmarked for relatives, lovers, or "loyal pupils" (an equally wayward yet widely used category), or with state funds going to private universities of every type and location: a squandering of public money of which too little is said. But are we to create poverty simply in order to avoid theft? The reference to ethics is highly complex and problematic, not least because it puts its finger on the wound: the social and moral value of merit is part and parcel of a Protestant ethic from which liberalism, which is not only a political order, has taken shape. In a celebrated work by John Calvin, *The Institutes of the Christian Religion,* talents and merits are theorized as the foundations of Christian justice: of the duty of each person—not redeemable through prayer or the enactment of the practices commanded—to express what the Creator has given them. Nonetheless, this insistence upon individual merit, and upon the responsibility of the community to nurture it and to respect it, is not as rooted in Catholic tradition or, at any rate, not in so pronounced a fashion: it represents rather a central component of the ethic of modernity. It would, however, be an error to argue in a fatalistic fashion. We must view liberal democracy as an order that is not solely procedural since it is also a form of society, a society's mode of existence, as Tocqueville had clearly seen, and not only a method for selecting representatives and for taking collective decisions. And ethics is not a moral or subjective fact but designates a mode of operation of social, cultural, and political institutions whereby each sector of society has a direct and reciprocal influence upon the others. An ethos that sustains merit is a way of proceeding coordinated between a training system and the system of the labor market, but it is also a factor of recognition. It is based upon individual responsibilities and capacities as well as upon the impact of others' opinions upon our choices. It is a broad ethos that holds society and all its component parts together: from politics to the family, from civil society to the economy. This, for example, entails society being so organized that the university forms knowledgeable students rather than simply many graduates (yet Italian law considers the quantity of students who graduate as a criterion by which to decide the quantity of resources to be distributed). This is primed to encourage the university to recruit good lecturers.

Ability and commitment should, in other words, prove advantageous to those who strive to put them into practice and to the whole educational and labor system. Which is why sectorial reforms do not suffice if one wishes merit to be recognized and paid for. We need to pay attention to the whole system and not just to sectorial interventions.

6

Differences and Identity Politics

Q. One of the mutations of democracy—as we said earlier—is its tendency to assume ever more identitary connotations. Suppose we take a step back: how are we to define identity? And when did identity enter the political debate?

A. The politics of identity started to become relevant when traditional ideologies began to decline. Because of their all-embracing character, those ideologies have often been lived in an almost religious guise, creating identities of belonging rendered still more powerful by symbolic representations. Ideological identities, as well as being characterized by a doctrinaire Manichaeism, were the protagonists of the Cold War, itself an extraordinary symbolic and identitary "creation." The socialist or communist ideal, for example, or even the liberal-democratic ideal of American inspiration (by which I mean the "religion of liberty" pitted against communist "barbarism"), designated a set of values and conceptions as to how to organize society and even how to conduct one's private life. As unit-ideas they were immediately recognizable thanks to some specific symbols, such as the flags and the hymns, the slogans and even the modes of dress, and finally the two emblematic representative countries, which were, so to speak, role models and sources of inspiration.

For those who recognized themselves in them, these ideological entities were like sites of solidarity akin to villages or churches: sites that made each feel a part of a common project—and above all of a project whose presuppositions were incontestably good. The parties embodying such ideologies were ethical worlds that held together people who were different in several respects yet united in the name of something that transcended them all and that was more important than any motive for being different. The unity of interpretation and of values constituted the common character with respect to which differences entailed if anything enrichment rather than confrontation. To use Anne Phillips's idiom, the "politics of ideas" was more important than the "politics of presence" because it more effectively included claims based on cultural or gender identity within a broader narrative of emancipation and social justice. Women, workers, students, or peasants were not supposed to vaunt their specificity in order not to suffer discrimination or injustices: in those ideologies, indeed, there was a place for everyone, provided that no one claimed a visibility independently of the others and the encompassing unity. They offered an answer to every problem and to every circumstance, in some way simplifying the complexity of social existence and at the same time furnishing secure orientations for the assessment of problems and for their possible solution.

This all-encompassing world of representative values and ideals entered into crisis when the two role-model countries ceased to exist in that antagonistic relationship. Although the politics of civil rights, which played an important role also in European countries (Italy in particular), had already started to erode ideological identifications by stressing the role of the individual, her choice and liberty, the end of the Cold War marked a turning point so far as a broad spectrum of social and political issues were concerned. We have to keep in mind that in Europe the construction of the welfare state was led by political parties that became mass parties during the Cold War. The welfare state was sustained, as we have said previously, by citizens who were organized into parties and trades unions and whose ideological language pivoted around the central figure of the citizen-worker. A factor by no means of secondary importance in this crisis has been the actual process of stabilization of democracy, which—we should recall—does not promise the realization of the ideal city. Yet socialism and liberalism are nonetheless ideologies that devise some specific goals, whereas democracy promises essentially an equal share in the political power of determining or influencing the government, and without dictating any particular goal for which that power should be used, save reproducing the democratic process and its foundations. In short, the secularization of the political religions was both the effect of a historical fact (the end of the Cold War) and the consequence of democracy's stabilization, which has left the parties not only denuded of symbols but also anachronistic in relation to the premises and promises of democracy. This process of political secularization has revealed the nonutopian face of democracy, a political system that erodes ideological identities and the representative power of palingenetic ideals.

Thus, in the 1960s, in the United States and shortly afterward in Europe, we witnessed the gradual assertion of and demand for new forms of representation and identification, this time not for general or ideal reasons, nor for party aggregations. Differences, as it were, have disassociated themselves from the whole and claim their own autonomous visibility. Consequently, citizens have become the agents of their own vindication, without the mediation of the party; "presence" has gradually got the upper hand over "ideas." Difference has become a justification for associating, allying, and uniting, prompting solidarity and the clustering together of those who were different from others in some aspect they considered to be relevant.

The first challenge within the ideology of the Left and social-democratic political culture was launched by the "New Left," and it was no longer in the name of the integration of citizenship into the collective body (after all, social-democratic ideology had hoped to achieve this kind of political inclusion when stressing the centrality of labor). Now citizens started being mobilized in the name of a specific liberation, one that was more cultural and social than political.

Q. *However, feminism has been a pacesetter where the birth of the politics of difference is concerned.*

A. Having a job, according to the "New Left" (in Italy the Left outside the PCI and the PSI, that is, outside the communist and socialist parties, although in a short space of time these ideas went on to penetrate every party and movement), did not constitute a factor of liberation save when it was accompanied by civil gains, relating for example to the private dimension of choice, such as procreation and sexual freedom. The demand for just redistribution was no longer felt to be sufficient:

it was necessary to acquire the right to the recognition of one's own specific difference precisely as women or, in the United States, as African Americans or homosexuals. The struggle for civil rights had the power to exalt the centrality of the subjective sphere (that of individual choices and preferences) over the political and the social.

If the social-democratic ideologies had proposed that liberty be read as a good requiring some social conditions or opportunity, the mode of argument was now reversed: civil liberty and civil rights constituted the primary condition of liberty, in relation to which social goods were just one factor. There thus arose the first great challenge to the democratic universalism of policies deemed to be just because they sought to neutralize differences. The demand for the freedom to enter the public sphere with one's own cultural or gender identities became the language of the new politics of emancipation and of the struggle for recognition. Generalist ideas yielded to ideas of difference and began to be seen as synonymous with the defense of the status quo. Democracy, this was the new argument, is not simply a system of procedures and institutions. Rather it is a way of participating or of seeking representation in the public arena of the differences belonging to citizens. Ideas of right, law, and universality thus changed their meaning.

Social justice notwithstanding—Iris Marion Young has written—women are not equal citizens, for a reason that is not only economic or a matter of legal equality. Nor is it for a reason that is negative. Women citizens are political actors who are of a specific gender, and they are not "simply" citizens, nor do they want to be or become "simply" citizens. Consequently, equal laws and the courts applying them impartially are not sufficient, nor does the distribution of social services in support of working women suffice: if a condition of discrimination is a cultural fact, if it depends upon the specific situation in which those discriminated against happen to find themselves, it then becomes necessary to go beyond the universalism of norms and procedures—since a universalism of that kind does not enable us to see that it is in the nonrecognition of difference that the cause of injustice lies. It is necessary to tear off the veil of neutrality in order to reveal what lies beneath, namely, a social world full of differences.

The critique of horizontal equality and of procedural democracy advance together and have been conducted in the name of a democracy more alert to the informal sphere of civil society and the concrete circumstances of women and of men in their private, not only in their social, domains: hence the demand that, for justice to be realized, differences must not be ignored but in fact highlighted, starting with those of gender and sexual preference, so as to accord them moral and juridical recognition.

Q. *Have you answered my question about identity yet? What is it? How would you define it?*

A. Group identity is conditional on representation, on the recognition of a group of persons by others and beforehand by the members of the group, in relation to an element that is not the immediate consequence of individual choice but in fact determines the choice of the individuals. Identity unites and differentiates at one and the same time, and it is not a given but a construction through a representative process of attribution and self-attribution of specificity and meaning. We can translate it—and it has often been translated—into a reason for discrimination by those who are in the political or cultural majority, for whom being a woman has, for example, entailed having fewer resources in order to compete in economic and social life, in career and work and in politics. As Nancy Fraser has argued, identity is barely comprehensible if disassociated from recognition and power distribution. Yet we may say, even more radically, that identity is essentially a question of representation.

Gender identity is highly artificial and constructed; it does not of course stem from nature and does not depend upon being a member of the female sex (apart from anything else, technology has also rendered this "naturalness" an artificial thing). It depends rather upon the wider culture, social and moral; upon power relations between the two sexes, within the family and outside of it; upon the management of social and political power; and, above all, upon the symbolic representation of women and men, hence upon education and the reproduction of the relevant roles and social values. Baby girls and baby boys learn to live in the fashion that society thinks that women and men should relate to one another. And from the language and codes of conduct one can infer the manner in which the distribution of power between men and women occurs, or, rather, how men organize the power that women then interiorize and to which they adapt. The aim of this work of socialization is for the position that men and women occupy in society to appear to the protagonists themselves to be a natural fact and thus to be accepted without discussion and without the sense of resentment that would stem from nursing even just a slight suspicion that one was the victim of a trick. Gender relations are thus the mirror of a hegemonic culture that lives in the mind and through the behavior of persons and that shapes their lives with their own conscious participation. As said before, this identity construction has to remain impervious to critical examination in order to be accepted fully by persons, and there is no better way to achieve this result than to present it as a natural fact or as the outcome of a series of natural conditions. Equality of conditions would in this case come to mean that each person does what by "nature" they are deputed to do. This has been for centuries the popular philosophy that has justified inequality between the sexes.

The critique of this upside-down vision of equality and of difference is not meant to sustain the view that women are better or worse human beings than men: it is not the moral judgment that should concern us here but the judgment of power relations. For centuries the social and public life of women has been modeled upon the role they have in the reproduction of the species, a role that, without their consent, has been used to exclude them from the world of social and political choices. And above all, these power relations prepared them mentally to accept their own position, forever and ever, even when, in the happiest of hypotheses, they manage to become social protagonists. As Simone de Beauvoir has written, they are educated from the time they were little girls to play the affective, erotic, and social roles that domestic life with the other sex provides for, requires, and expects. Within this upside-down philosophy, political emancipation itself and the emancipation of rights can be used to sustain the natural inequality of women: as Lawrence Summers, then president of Harvard University, said a few years ago, their having had political and civil rights has not erased the fact that women are nonetheless "unequal" (meaning "inferior") in cognitive potential. If despite decades of emancipation women are "different" from men in regard to such basic achievements, is it perhaps not a confirmation that women are "different"? Is it perhaps not true that the culture of rights has done justice to what was thought to be an effect of social discrimination and meanwhile shows what the real nature of woman is? That, in short, women, though having had the option of leading a professional and public life, continue to be suited to domestic life? What better proof could there be of the naturalness of our "difference" (or "inferiority") than free choice?

There is no worse sign of subordination than what is experienced by those women who, although having won social and political roles, feel that they are never treated like their male fellow citizens. At any rate, their so-called equality is shown to be a sham, their power, their methods, their style, and their appearance all being found wanting: it is not sufficient to do the same work as men to be seen and treated in as dignified a fashion as the men treat one another. For this reason too, wishing to be "like" men is a losing game—and a humiliating one at that. Representative and symbolic power is carried by recognition, which as ever rests on equality: we seek the recognition of equals. But which equality? As we have said, it can readily be interpreted as equality of equals and not as a relation of equal consideration between those who are different.

To be perfectly honest, I do not believe that our having equal rights leads to our being accepted as equals by men and by social institutions. Nor do I think that "acceptance" should be the objective because that would involve a recognition of authority vested in the person whose acceptance one sought, instead of equality. And again, how can one fail to see that the men who gather at symposiums and seminars never pay any heed to the fact that they are exclusively men or that when there are women there are always very few of them? How is one to account for men's blindness toward gender difference? And how can one fail to see that being a part of the world of culture is in no way sufficient for achieving recognition of equality of dignity?

It seems to me that a subterranean cause underlies the inequality of power: women have not yet managed to win the right to speak out about reproductive power. Their social and political subjection will continue for so long as they are deprived of the authority of choice over the mastery of life, that is, over the reproduction of the species, in that context of power which is the most fateful in the construction of social roles. Women have not the power to rule over the life that they cause to be born. They have been and are still put in the state of being a gestating uterus, not engenderers of life. Undoubtedly it is in the birth of life that the force upon which the power of women is gambled lies—and civil and political rights are a means to attain to this power. Those skeptical about democracy have good reason to think that the right to vote has not radically changed things. Nonetheless, it has precipitated the protest, and changes are underway. Gender difference started to matter once women began to understand the nature of this unique power relationship that not even the declaration of rights has managed to touch. The politics of difference has been to all intents and purposes a revolution, one never completed and always in progress. And it has been such not despite political rights but thanks to them.

Q. The theme of "identity" differs from that of "difference": what implications does identity have for democratic politics?

A. Let us take the case of religion. Believing in a God is certainly a factor that unites and differentiates. I would not wish to be misunderstood here: the centrality of the religious foundation of politics is far from new. The novelty lies in its rebirth on the political stage of the constitutional democracies. When identity by virtue of faith seeks to have a political voice and a public presence, religious specificity risks becoming a serious danger for the rule of law, for tolerance, and therefore also for democracy. The modern state was born in part through the exclusion of religions from the sphere of political power: by freeing political power from religions, it freed that power from violence and intolerance for reasons of faith.

With the adoption of charters of rights, and therefore with the recognition of a limit to the power of the majority, the democracies have rendered the old toleration anachronistic and unjust: religious liberty is a fundamental principle that frees conscience from every secular authority and, if necessary, from the clergy also—it would be better to say from every authority external to the conscience of persons who are responsible and therefore free. Individual rights render toleration a question of individual conduct and no longer a state politics. Defending the rights of everyone to freedom is truly an advance upon the discretional decision of the state to tolerate this or that faith.

Q. During these recent years in which the ideological religions have declined, we have witnessed the rebirth of the theological religions.

A. It is not so much a rebirth in the sense of the reappearance of the religious or faith phenomenon, which has never been in decline, as the mounting presence of religious identity (indeed, of the religious hierarchies that represent that identity) in the public sphere of the democratic societies, a presence intent upon changing codes and laws. It is a rebirth that does not lay claim to a specific liberty—because every citizen enjoys the liberty to manifest their own religious credo before others and to practice their own religion in designated sites—but calls for a special presence of the reasons of the faith (of its representatives) in political contexts, for example, in public decision making. It calls for the precedence of religious over political identity, which is often conceived as an instrument in the service of that same precedence.

Those advancing this claim think that every context of life is and should be accessible to faith and moreover that religious faith is a source of authority in moral conduct of superior value. In short, the politics of (religious) identity challenges the liberal idea that one should endeavor to keep the spheres of civil and religious life separate, despite knowing, as I have just explained, that separation will not necessarily bring happiness and an end to conflict; indeed, that it is itself the object of bargaining and compromise and thus anything but easy. The objective of happiness is, and remains, ethical. It can't be assumed by a magistrate or by the law, on pain of curtailing freedom and transforming the state from a state of right into an ethical, confessional, or simply paternalistic state. The politics of religious identity contests the principle of separation and differentiation, which is precisely why I think we should be worried.

Q. *There are other examples of the politics of identity, for example, those defending a specific ethnic or linguistic identity against being absorbed by the language and culture of the majority. One can legitimately ask oneself whether the law should set out to protect cultural or ethnic minorities.*

A. There is an abundant literature on this question, known as the theory of multiculturalism. My concern here is to underline its political repercussions. In my opinion, it is principally a matter of prudence: there are cases in which it is prudent for a national community to adopt specific policies for national groups or communities that are numerically in the minority, above all if and when they are geographically concentrated in a particular territory.

This is the case with the Italian resolution of the conflict with the German majority living in the subregion of South Tyrol, who have fought for some decades, sometimes violently, for secession. This involved a minority so far as the national territory was concerned, but that minority was a strong community (and actually a majority) in a part of the country that was calling for guarantees of its survival, so to speak, and that has made significant gains, beginning with reserved seats (quotas) in parliament for their representatives, bilingualism in public examinations for official jobs and in regional offices, and, finally, a large measure of regional administrative autonomy with very generous financial support by the central state. These campaigns emanating from the South Tyrol represented demands that the central state help halt the decline of a minority national identity: an attempt at protection and self-defense. The South Tyrolean minorities are of course concentrated in one region; if they had been scattered over the whole national territory, it would have been difficult for them to pursue an identity politics of self-government.

Q. In the United States, as I have already intimated, the question of identity has been bound up with that of affirmative action, that is to say, with those policies originally introduced in the 1960s to attenuate, through preferential measures of support, the historical effects of discrimination in its various forms: gender, race, religion, sexual orientation, country of origin.

A. Yes, and after the social policies promoted by the Lyndon B. Johnson administration there was in the private sector the change of direction of AT&T in 1973, when the telecommunications multinational decided to advertise for secretarial posts, thirty-two of which would be reserved for members of minorities, that is, for women and African Americans. Some political philosophers—in particular Will Kymlika—have sought to argue that liberalism can be configured in such a way that, on the one hand, it preserves some universal rights equally accessible to all individually and, on the other hand, that it satisfies cultural rights because of the need to protect a community or a cultural or ethnic minority.

When fundamental individual rights are not violated, it is possible to grant minorities spaces of self-government or of self-regulation that take their cultural specificity or their religious tradition into account.

A cultural right is, for example, a criterion that suggests a local government should adopt a norm enabling shopkeepers of Muslim faith to carry out their common activities in accordance with their—and not our—religious practices. We are concerned here with prudential solutions since, if individual right is fundamental and should remain such, accommodations occur in relation to questions that are not essential for the fundamental rights although they are of practical and even moral concern for individuals. It is possible to have a broad politics of cultural rights, but the decision regarding its breadth should be taken by the "wider" political community and not by the cultural group that sustains it, holding firm to the defense of individual rights, which are not always in harmony with the defense of the community that demands cultural policies respectful of its own identity or tradition. While civil rights are not negotiable, cultural policies are, and for this reason they can always be revoked, and they remain subject to the will of the political majority. It seems to me that, precisely for this reason, multiculturalism is above all a prudential politics, that is, an expedient that does not undermine the liberal system. Otherwise it would be a challenge to the state of right and a new version of the corporative state.

Q. *What role does identity have in the great mutation of which we are speaking?*

A. The politics of identity and the recognition of difference are not the same thing. The latter means that the law, in order to treat all fairly and equally, is applied in such a way that the factors of difference are not translated into discrimination or unequal treatment. In many cases, as we have seen, if the law does not pay heed to the concrete circumstances of citizens, it ends up being unjust, losing the very thing it lays claim to, namely, neutrality. This applies in the first instance to social policies. Impartiality becomes an empty formalism if it limits itself to being blind to the specific conditions that can translate into injustice and require attention to the context; in these cases what is called neutrality risks being a graph of the point of view of the group with the power to establish the conditions of "normality."

Contemporary liberal theorists tend to attribute to liberalism a status *super partes* in order to expunge reasons for contestation and disagreement from public debate. They seek to ascribe to the liberal structure of society a neutral character and status, so as to defend it from partisan claims arising from strong or religious conceptions of the good and from metaphysical visions of the good life liable to unleash intolerance and to put the stability of the state and society at risk. Though such an attribution may be prudent and reasonable with regard to *certain* types of "conception of the good," it is not valid for all of them, and it cannot be extended in the same manner and indiscriminately to every institution or every citizen. It is reasonable to wonder whether the notion of neutrality applies equally to religious and cultural perfectionism on the one hand and, on the other, to questions relating to the concrete opportunities individuals may have to pursue their projects.

Theories of neutrality obscure the fact that liberalism does itself have a perfectionist kernel because its criterion of validation puts at the center, and in an unequivocal fashion, the individual, her dignity, and her equal consideration as a person. As regards the social or cultural position or economic class in which a person happens to find herself, the liberal conception, if interpreted in this perfectionist sense, may therefore suggest or provoke partisanship. The paradox of the philosophy of neutrality is that it cannot ignore the prevailing conditions of discrimination and injustice for fear of losing validity; nonetheless, recognizing such conditions necessarily requires renouncing neutrality or, to be more precise, circumscribing it. The laws should not tell us either to worship or how to worship God (or gods) nor whether, how, and whom to love. But the consensus as to what the state should not do becomes more precarious and open to contestation when it is a question of the basic conditions (material and cultural) of individual well-being. For example, liberalism can legitimately prompt us to think that the state should not be neutral as regards the choice parents make not to send their children to school, or the length of the working day, or the minimal material conditions for individual life and liberty.

Finally, the decision as to *where* one should apply, ratify, and safeguard neutrality is no less controversial. Is the quest for impartiality as appropriate to the case of a politician or a deputy as it is to that of a judge or a civil servant? What is the place of neutrality in legislative decisions, in which parties, interests, values, and ideas hold the bank? In addition, are we to suppose that an individual citizen behaves or should behave like a judge or a civil servant when she places her voting slip in the ballot box or that she should give an impartial justification for her political choices?

The wisdom of those applying the law has an important role. Bobbio wrote that social rights are born in order to so arrange matters that political and civil rights are enjoyed without discrimination against those who are not equal. For example, it would be a very bad law that considered maternity to be an illness, maintaining that, otherwise, only women would enjoy the right to take time off work: this was an argument I heard defended at a university seminar, in the name of justice construed as impartiality.

The law cannot disregard difference nor therefore treat maternity as an illness on the grounds that it does not affect men as well. It can if need be recognize maternity leave for the father also, and when it does this it not only delivers more equality to citizens, women and men alike, but also has positive ethical effects because it induces parents to think of themselves as equals in the distribution of familial sacrifices and commitments.

One can cite numerous instances of regulations that are unjust because they are falsely neutral. Before gender difference was recognized in the workplace and by the unions, the job descriptions of the professions and of the manual trades were conceived and written on the basis of the capacities and attributes of the male body. In this case, treating everyone equally meant treating everyone, women and men, as if they were male. False universality, or the blindness of the law when faced with disadvantageous circumstances produced by social relations, confirms injustice instead of correcting it.

However, the politics of difference does not only have a role that is negative, that is to say, one of supervising, denouncing, and transforming the laws in force. It can also be an assertion of power as identity politics: for example, when a group lays claim to its own specificity against the majority and against other groups, asking that politics follow identity and that the law be modeled upon the most representative or majoritarian identity within a given territory. This happens when the identity groups represent themselves not so much or not solely as different but as deserving of a power or a consideration greater than those of other groups. When these identity groups loom large in a region and acquire the electoral power to make decisions, they can then assert themselves as a power group: the north to the Po Valley people, the south to the southerners, as if all those in either were wholly identical, or as if north and south were inhabited by internally homogeneous ethnic groups.

Q. Why do you find it so alarming a phenomenon?

A. When the majority of the population in a region or a territory declares itself to be identical in something that is not transferable or extendable through law to all—and from this point of view dialect is no less discriminatory than skin color, being hard to learn so well that one is not recognized as a foreigner—it can become dangerous, because that majority is tempted to use the law in a discriminatory fashion, excluding or treating in an arbitrary way those who belong to the minority. An example? The Northern League mayors in some small towns in the Italian northeast who took it upon themselves to decide whether the children of immigrants could attend nursery schools or if they should be subject to oppressive rules.

Q. In the Italian political context, has the Northern League assumed the identitary connotations to which you refer?

A. I do not believe that all those who voted for the Northern League are the same. The Northern League is not an ethnicity but a political party, and the "North of the Po Valley" imagined as a region with the attributes of a homogeneous nation is an invention devised to reward a political class. I want to insist on this point: northern Italy is not a territory inhabited by an ethnically or culturally homogeneous group. This is truly a fiction that the high-flown rhetoric of a party of minoritarian origin has rendered overwhelming. We must avoid repeating in reverse the errors that we are criticizing. Yet by means of propaganda and money, the Northern League has for years presented itself as the representative of all the Italians of the north, and it has made itself the bearer of a communitarian and even racist philosophy. Having in their hands some levers of power at this regional administrative level and for some years even at the national level, this communitarian party has maintained and maintains still that its task is simply to satisfy the demands of the citizens of "Padania," that is to say, of their electors, all but forgetting that members of parliament do not represent only the citizens who voted for them but the whole nation. Ethnic identitary politics endorses discriminatory measures and in addition becomes, as we see daily, a passport to corruption: if the higher good is the interest of one's own group, why not use public money to feather one's nest? In this circumstance identitary politics is radically illiberal, apart from being a negation of the principle of the state of right in the name of a private principle, such as the good of one's own friends in the party or the particular traditions of a group of apartment blocks or communes.

Gianfranco Miglio, one of the inspirations behind the regionalist and federalist rhetoric of the Northern League, was an antiliberal who held that politics was an assertion of identity. Having studied Carl Schmitt, being indeed an admirer of his thought, Miglio applied the category friend/enemy to the construction of the Northern League as political subject. This took its first steps at the end of the 1970s, after the birth of regional governments (thanks to the new law passed in 1970). The Northern League emerged as an expression of regionalism just when the Christian-Democratic hegemony went into decline in areas of the northeast that were on the lookout for a new political representation able to manage local power and the distribution of benefits. Even the reinforcement of the European Union and its regionalist policies, which served to counterbalance the power of the central states of the member countries, has contributed despite itself to the strengthening of regionalist parties with ideologies of ethnic homogeneity.

Q. *You speak of a mutation of democracy in an identitary sense. How would you define this process?*

A. It is what I have just said when referring to a group of persons who, for the most disparate reasons, deem it legitimate to use the law to advance their own interests at the expense of everyone else. The free marketeers often cite the Danish case as a success story, pointing to the dismantling of the welfare state and to liberalizations and privatizations stimulating employment. But they do not specify that the reform of the labor market on the Danish model does not apply in that country to foreign workers, though they pay their taxes just like the Danes and are numerous. Even if we concede that it was a successful reform, it was achieved by discriminating against some workers and giving preferential treatment to others.

Q. There are thousands of similar cases in Italy.

A. Yes. For example, in the administering of social services. Are they reserved for Italian citizens, or are they extended to those who work, pay their taxes, and, though not Italian, live in the same territory? By airing such arguments, populist candidates won several local elections in the last twenty years. Immigrants from non-European countries, assuming that they work and pay their taxes, should have the selfsame rights as an Italian citizen who was born in the same street or even in the same house in which her family had lived for generations. If European states welcome foreigners, it is because their economies need their labor, and they allow them entry with a work permit. Since these workers contribute to the social good just like everyone else, they must have the use of the same services—unless, that is, citizenship is to be interpreted as ethnicity. And in truth Italian law, regulating voting rights for Italian citizens resident abroad, takes this identitary principle for granted, because giving a passport and the right to vote to Italians born abroad as long as four generations ago means maintaining that in Italy citizenship follows the criterion not of soil but of blood.

Q. Do you reckon all identities to be equal?

A. No. There are those who, for example, seek to become powerful in order to dominate a territory because they are in the majority, and there are those who, like the South Tyrolese, are endeavoring not to disappear (even if I fear that these latter, if they in their turn became a majority, would themselves lord it over their minorities). The furthest point of the struggle for power is reached when the majoritarian group in a territory struggles for secession. If an ethnic group with a strong identitary culture, and perhaps a language and a religion different from the national ones, instead of being scattered across the whole territory of a country, happens to be concentrated in a single region, it could pose serious problems for the integrity of the national unit. Dispersion across a territory enables the members of identity groups to place more trust in the individual rights that the state guarantees, even against the majority of that same group.

We should bear in mind that rights do not serve the majority but those who are in the minority, that is to say, those who are weaker, in order to protect themselves from the strong (most of the time those who are in the majority). In Italy, a Muslim who wishes to pray in a mosque lays claim to a just and constitutional right. Often, however, at the local level Muslim communities are not authorized to build places of worship because the region, the province, or the commune, having responsibility for town planning, will block proposals for unavowed discriminatory motives. "No one is preventing Muslims from praying," we often hear it said, "but for reasons of public order we do not wish the mosque to be visible." Faced with these justifications, citizens of the Muslim faith have a sacrosanct right to appeal to the Italian constitution and to ask for equal consideration, in the name of the right to worship freely, which means the right to practice a faith, not only the right to believe.

Q. *What happens when the majority imposes its conception of identity?*

A. In a society that hinges upon a constitution and equal rights, no identity should of itself count for more than any other. On the other hand, identitarian politics proclaims the intention of creating a society that is composed of the same people and of distributing equal rights among only the equals in something more than simply the law. In the Europe of the twentieth century there have been several examples of this form of totalitarian appropriation of rights and the law. I don't think identity politics of a totalitarian kind belongs only to the past. Neofascist movements and ethnically based populisms are emerging in several European states. Although it may seem they have accepted the democratic rules of the game, there are reasons to doubt their constitutional sincerity. It happened in the past that when they won majorities in liberal parliaments they changed the political identity of their states and implemented their identitarian projects.

Q. *Is there a link between identitary mutation and racist degenerations?*

A. Racisms, in the form in which they are known to us in Europe, are often the offshoots of nationalisms. In the mid–nineteenth century, race became a category with scientific pretensions, and anthropology departments devoted to the study of race emerged. Alongside those who maintained that there is just the one human species there were those who, in a ostensibly scientific manner, began to argue that different races originally existed. The unitary vision of the human species had been challenged by, for example, Joseph Arthur de Gobineau, a French author who, attributing distinct physiological, moral, and psychological characteristics to each race, maintained that the mixing of the races led to their being weakened. Through refusing mixture, whites and blacks alike could maintain their purity and vigor. Nonetheless, it would be absurd and simplistic to argue that identitary politics and cultures always pave the way for racist regressions. This is not what I would maintain.

Q. *Do you see the identitary mutation as a global phenomenon affecting every democracy, or is it restricted to the European continent?*

A. Europe is perhaps the most fertile and dangerous terrain for phenomena of this kind. The reasons are many and complex, but there is no doubting the fact that there is strong resistance in Europe to accepting pluralism. It is, moreover, an ancient crux: consider the violence with which Christian unity was defended before and above all after the Reformation. The ideal of Christian concord that was reinforced, after Luther's disobedience, both among Catholics and among Protestants, was not intended to be a pacific concession to pluralism. Quite the reverse. If the pluralism of those in "error" came to be accepted by Protestants and Catholics, it was in the hope of correcting that error and therefore overcoming or diluting pluralism. As the historian Mario Turchetti has documented, in Europe pluralism was for centuries held to be a negative model of coexistence, one identified with "pluralist" empires reckoned to be a bad model of politics, such as the Roman and Ottoman empires.

From the nineteenth century onward, the impetus toward unity and uniformity assumed the guise of the nation, in which differences were tolerated rather than accepted, in the hope of a fusion or a complete assimilation. The American sequence has been different although not immune to nationalism or to the myth of "fusionism." Yet the United States was not born of a national project but rather of political emancipation: in any case, the colonies were autonomous and in no way disposed to merge themselves in a unitary national project. In Europe, democracy has been like a tree planted in the terrain of the nation and through a political revolution imposed from above by narrow elites. In America, the democratic project was born before the national one: the federation was a unitary project subsequent to rebellion against the British masters—a project that spoke the language of republican liberty and pluralism.

Q. Pluralism is at the center of many lines of enquiry. There are those who think that the ambiguities surrounding its role are growing and that this leads to a degeneration that is reflected even in democracy and in the great mutation of which we are speaking.

A. I want to illustrate the theme of pluralism by recalling a case that is perhaps not entirely representative but that raises interesting, tricky, and in some respects even grave questions as to our way of interpreting pluralism. It has to do with the motivation behind the decision of the court in Bologna in the summer of 2011 not to entrust to social services a Roma child whom the family did not wish to send to school. The little girl, who lived with her parents in the province of Parma (a northern city, economically very prosperous), attended school very irregularly. Social services intervened, and the police ascertained that she was living in squalor, with a family often at odds with the justice system and involved in petty crime. The public prosecutor responsible for minors, Ugo Pastore, and the Court of Appeal in Bologna found that they were speaking two different languages, with the former invoking equal rights, the latter "juridical pluralism." For Prosecutor Pastore, "Roma conditions" required that the law intervene on the little girl's behalf; for Bologna's Court of Appeal, that same context exempted her from compulsory attendance at school and the authorities from having to force the parents to send her there. Citing the norms safeguarding the rights of minors, from the New York Convention to the Italian penal code, Prosecutor Pastore had requested that the little girl be sent to school against the will of her parents. The division of the Bologna Court of Appeal responded as follows: "The nomadic circumstances and the actual culture of origin do not lead us to suppose that harm will be done to the minor." There was no proof of "conduct on the part of the parents inconsistent with the normal way of life in terms of circumstances and origin."

According to this mode of reasoning, law should follow mores, that is to say, tradition and culture. It should halt at the threshold of the church, of traditions, and of communities, as if acknowledging that the latter are the primary goods that the law must protect, rather than the dignity of the person, especially when that person is not capable of asserting their own reasons, as is the case with a minor. One cannot help but see the contradiction in this argument. It would be as if,

given that a few decades ago it was usual for Italian parents to beat their
✓ children, the law should have respected that practice, its naturalness
rendering it harmless.

It seems that for the Court of Appeal in Bologna it is the ethical context that determines the scope of the norm. This mode of reasoning is unfortunately less and less exceptional, and it constitutes a justification for juridical pluralism that establishes a priority, namely, that of the communitarian culture and of the local environment over civil law and its universality. And it is another eloquent sign of the struggle between the two principles: that of force—it matters little whether it is called tradition, honor, or economic power—and that of right. I invite you to ponder this tension when I speak of the mutation as a decline in the culture of equality and of the dignity of the person.

Q. It seems as if the episode of the little Roma girl confirms a phenomenon, ever more frequent, whereby identitary belonging is invoked as a principle that precedes individual right.

A. Nonpolitical belonging or identity often becomes a value having priority over persons. The logic appears back to front: since the identity of persons is defined by the contexts, it is these latter that are the real good to be defended. This is the ideology that fosters the conviction that equality should only apply to equals. Preaching identitary equality (whereby every group of equals has its own equality) entails negating equality as a principle of relationship between the different. By this I do not mean to suggest that persons are like monads without bonds between them and without contexts. It is important to me rather to highlight the fact that behind this vision privileging context one can discern an insidious challenge to universalism and to the value of the person. Those who believe in the primary value of the community maintain that if we interrogate individual actions and beliefs from the point of view of their fidelity to rights, we ultimately end up questioning their loyalty to modes of belonging and constitutive values, such as the family, cultural traditions, and religious affiliations. This is the identitary alternative to the universalism of rights, and as an argument it is more than insidious.

Q. If it is so, it is perhaps because it seeks to convince us that, if we really hold to the individual, we must respect the culture from which that individual comes?

A. It is assumed that the individual is the product of the context in which she lives, indeed, that she is what the context is and is its microcosm. We are concerned here—as one may easily intuit—with a perspective that nails personal identity to a reality that precedes it, that will continue after it, and that for this reason has more importance than the individual biography itself. This mode of reasoning is pernicious because, while it claims to contest and transcend individualism, it overturns and puts first what lasts or persists, that is to say, not our personal life, which is short, shorter, indeed, than traditions and communities. On the other hand, this life of mine and of yours, here and now, is the good that the theory and practice of rights protects even, if necessary, against the bond of the cultural context.

That nonelective (and in this sense irrational) nucleus that we call tradition (or community) is certainly not reducible to relations based upon right and upon the general norm. The ethical life of affective relationships is not reducible to rights, nor is it the sum of individual choices. Let us consider an exemplary instance of ethical life, namely, marriage. Which is not only the marriage contract, nor is it reducible to it. Married life ceases to be an ethical world when wife and husband need to appeal to the law to restore the dimension of respect to their relations and when the affective relationship is no longer capable of autonomously holding together their respective wills and desires. Then it is that respect, which had first been engendered by love, has to be obtained through the law, indeed, imposed by the law. The fact of needing laws establishes that marriage as ethical experience has ended, whereas marriage as contract is as much in evidence as ever. However, it is not only the affective relationship and the dimension of ethical life that gives value to a person but also the juridical relationship, which restores and reestablishes dignity and reciprocity when these latter no longer arise spontaneously through ethical life.

What is important to grasp is the fact that, without a doubt, ethical life may not be reduced to relationships of juridical respect: however, between ethical life and the life of right there is a relationship that is not one of opposition. The ethical life, that of the community, takes its inspiration from values that the rights and the laws incorporate abstractly, as for example reciprocity and respect. The marriage contract does not give identity to love or to solidarity: marriage or family are more than merely defined by the law. However, it would be mistaken to suppose that the ethical world is something other than law or actually superior to it. There is if anything an osmosis between the ethical life marked by erotic love, familial solidarity, and the life of the law: a relationship of correspondence whereby one mirrors the other. But this functions only for so long as there is no disagreement between the two worlds, between individual will and the ethical world of the family. When, however, tension arises, the juridical world rightly claims its priority because the good of the person comes first. It is here, then, that defending the rights of the individual does not mean adhering to an individualistic social vision or to a selfish philosophy. The law is respectful of the life of the community and safeguards in the abstract the principles of organization: it is so for so long as the ethical life can proceed on its own steam. Rights intervene—they should intervene—when the ethical life is compromised or the individual will does not reproduce it but avows a break between itself and the ethical life. This is why the reason of the law is a good to be preserved at all costs: on its sustainability rests the sustainability of the ethical life.

Q. *Undoubtedly, the reference to context helps explain the formation of our identity and of our values.*

A. But whenever it coincides with a philosophy that claims to account for our individual identity on the basis of the community and traditions, attention to context would translate as determinism, and from explanatory reason it would be transformed into metaphysical reason. I do not absolutely deny the cognitive and explanatory importance of the reference to context (of what is called "contextualism"). On the contrary, I think that knowledge of history, religion, literature, geography, and social and political institutions is crucial to our understanding the meaning of biography. And I share the critique of Enlightenment thought when it imposes itself as rationalistic metaphysics, because it would be a hindrance rather than an aid to our knowledge of social and ethical phenomena.

No action can be circumscribed in its implications to the person who performs it. In this sense everything that happens concerns us and has an impact upon us. This is true above all of political institutions, which are not created from nothing, nor do we find them already made as if they were pieces of stone, nor do we take them as perfect models from an ideal world and then impose them upon concrete reality. In short, context is an inescapable factor for understanding and meaning. But precisely for this reason law is necessary, since it must protect us from a context that is highly influential and cannot be either ignored or eliminated.

Q. The safeguarding of persons and of actual collectivities proceeds by way of the certainty of the law . . .

A. . . . a certainty given by laws that are general, transparent, and clear; democratically approved; defended by an efficient, impartial, and responsible administration; and protected by courts and magistrates called upon to formulate independent and impartial judgments, dismissing justificatory references to presumed entities of belonging, such as precisely a tradition or a system of values or an ethnicity. The fact of a little girl being born by chance into a Roma family cannot justify the priority of the tradition of the family over her interests in fashioning for herself a culture and a moral autonomy thanks to which she may decide, when she is an adult, whether to stay in that community or to leave.

Q. And it is a serious thing if a judge in a state founded upon law should endorse the opposite opinion.

A. When attention to context goes beyond the understanding of social phenomena and is expressed as a determinist philosophy of history that establishes values, the risk is that it will end up justifying what exists, promoting a cynical realism, that is, a recognition that the world of right is without value. A value that on the other hand only power—the power of tradition, of context, or of the community—would have. Certainly, we are children of our own time. No one is without a context, nor can she live in a rootless condition. But we become aware of this specific identity of ours through a critical examination of the context, an examination that transforms the milieu in which we happen to find ourselves into a milieu that we feel to be morally our own. Is this not anyway the reason why we carry our roots with us when we leave our original context? Context is not givenness: it is not a given fact or a condition that presents itself immediately to our consciousness, but it is an object of knowledge, analysis, recognition, and election on our part, one that is also freely accepted and in some cases freely refused.

Index

Bobbio, Norberto (*continued*)
90; militant democracy opposed
by, 95; patriotism and, 92; on
peace and liberty, 67; "politics of
dialogue" of, 93–94
Bologna, 31–32, 175–76
Burke, Edmund, 64

Calamandrei, Piero, 24, 139
Calvin, John, 155
Capital in the Twenty-First Century
(Piketty), 8–9
capitalism, 3, 16; democracy, compromise with, 106–8, 114–15;
without democracy, 134–35;
globalization and, 35–36; income
inequality and, 8–10; labor
compromise with, 115; laissez-
faire, 108; mutation of, 19; rise of
global, 18–19
Capitalism and Social Democracy
(Przeworski), 127
Catholicism, 137–38, 174
Chicago School, 115
Chilean coup of 1973, 99–100, 127
Christian Democratic Party (Italy),
60, 93
Christianity, 47
Churchill, Winston, 89, 114
Cicero, 63
citizenship: cosmopolitanism and,
7; as human right, 75; migrant
challenges with, 81–82; of stateless migrants, 75–76. *See also*
democratic citizenship
civil rights, 52, 59; cosmopolitan,
65–66; New Left and, 159–60
"civism," 87
Cleisthenes, 103–5
Clinton, Bill, 144–45

Codrignani, Giancarla, 140–41
Cohen, Jean L., 78
Cold War, 93–94, 134, 158
collective impoverishment, 10
Communist Manifesto, The (Marx
and Engels), 28, 121–22
communitarianism, ethnic, 87
conjectures, 40
Constituent Assembly, Italy, 23–24
consumerism, 19, 28
context, identity and, 176–79
contextualism, 178
continental model, of democratic
citizenship, 33–34
Convention Relating to the Status of
Stateless Persons, 73
cosmopolitanism: citizenship and, 7;
civil rights and, 65–66; EU and,
7; justice and, 65; liberty and,
64–65; nationalism and, 80; origin and vision of, 68; postnation,
76, 78; poststate, 75–76, 78; types
of, 8; universalism compared
to, 68–69. *See also* democratic
cosmopolitanism
cultural rights, 166–67

Dahl, Robert, 56
D'Alema, Massimo, 142
Darwinism, social, 108
de Condorcet, Marquis, 24, 69
De Gasperi, Alcide, 93
de Gobineau, Joseph Arthur, 173–74
deliberative democracy, 89–90,
94–95
democracy: alteration of, 19–20; in
ancient Greece, 102–6; antiegalitarian mutation of, 13–14, 17,
146–47; capitalism, compromise
with, 106–8, 114–15; capitalism

without, 134–35; challenges facing, 2–3, 34; creation of, 104; deliberative, 89–90, 94–95; economic power distribution and, 98, 101; equality and, 102–3, 136; ethos of, 88–90; in Europe following World War II, 114; free speech and, 53, 131; full employment and, 113, 127, 136; function of, 20; gated communities and, 32–33; goals and, 3–4, 20; habits and, 41–42; income inequalities and impact of, 14–15; individual as central to, 105; isonomic, 105–6; in Italy and Bobbio, 91–92; Italy and Cold War challenge for, 93–94; liberal, 15; liberalism compared to, 134; liberty and, 14–16, 103, 131; limitations of, 89; "many" and "few" compromise of, 102, 107, 130–31; Marx's skepticism towards, 135; militant, 95; mutation of, 3, 34, 53; Northern League and, 22–23; oligarchy in, 98–99; peace and, 106; pluralism and, 14; political freedom and, 4, 10–11; political power and, 5, 16; procedural, 160–61; public school as central to, 24; republicanism compared to, 133–34; Tocqueville on equality in, 48; Tocqueville on individualism and, 47; turning points in, 52–53; universalism and, 16; violence and, 88–89; during World War II, 135–36. *See also* representative democracy; social democracy

Democracy and Education (Dewey), 24

democratic citizenship, 5, 9; continental model of, 33–34; equality and, 17, 34, 101–2; EU and new, 72–73; hyphenated identities and, 33; Italy's broadening and tightening of, 27; labor and, 109–10; public reason for, 25; women and, 59–60

democratic cosmopolitanism: central presupposition of, 8, 68–69; civil society and politics in, 77–79; contradictions of, 77; EU and, 69, 86; globalization and, 71–72, 77; liberty and, 72; state and critique of, 78–79; stateless migrants and, 73

democratic justice, 56

demos, 103–4

Demosthenes, 150

Denmark, 171

Dewey, John, 24, 38–42, 149–50

Diamond, Larry, 100

difference, recognition of, 164, 167, 169

dignity, 95; labor and, 9; treating others with, 43

Discourse on the Origin and the Basis of Inequality Among Men (Rousseau), 4, 17

distributive justice, 115, 145–46, 149

divergence, forces of, 8–9

Dozza, Giuseppe, 32

economic independence, liberty and, 117

economic power: democracy and distribution of, 98, 101; of 1 percent, 100. *See also* income inequality elections, 53–54, 56–57. *See also* voting rights

Emerson, Ralph Waldo, 26

Engels, Friedrich, 28, 121–22

Enlightenment, 64, 91–92, 178

equality, 11; affirmative action and, 148–49; in ancient Greece, 105; as artificial construct, 16–17, 133; challenge of, 4; democracy and, 102–3, 136; democratic citizenship and, 17, 34, 101–2; diversity and, 51–52; equity compared to, 146; horizontal, 160–61; identity and, 172–73; ideologies and, 51; Italian public school and, 138; Italy and religious, 172–73; labor and, 110–11; liberty and, 46; merit and, 148–49, 151–52; as normative, 136; proportional, 150; representative democracy and, 55; Tocqueville on democracy and, 48; women's challenges with, 160–61. *See also* income inequality

equity, 145–46

ethical life, marriage and, 177–78

ethical state, 88

ethnic communitarianism, 87

ethnicity, 2, 11, 21, 170–71

ethnocentrists, rights and, 21–22

European Union (EU): cosmopolitanism and, 7; democratic cosmopolitanism and, 69, 86; executive dominance and, 86; human rights charter of, 84–85; identity of migrants and, 73; income inequality policies and opinions in, 127; legitimacy of, 86; multiculturalism and, 82; nationalism in, 21, 87; new demo-cratic citizenship and, 72–73; pluralism and, 174; possessive ideology in, 14; stateless migrants and, 73

exclusion politics, 2–3

executive dominance, EU and, 86

Falk, Richard, 8, 76

fascism, 24, 51, 80–81, 87, 92

fatalism, self-belief and, 43–45

"feminicide," 28

feminism, 159

"few": democracy as compromise of "many" and, 102, 107, 130–31; financial crisis of 2008, impact on, 122; "many," escalating tensions with, 100; tax cuts favoring, 118–19; "trickle-down" economics from, 123–25. *See also* oligarchy; 1 percent

fictions, necessity of, 42–43

financial capital, 132

financial crisis of 2008, 121–22

Fornero, Elsa, 147

Fortress America (Blakely), 29

fragmentation, 10–11

France, 33–34, 58, 83–85

Francis (Pope), 145

Fraser, Nancy, 161

free market, state advancing alongside, 18–19

free speech, democracy and, 53, 131

French Revolution, 46, 51

Friedman, Milton, 10, 115

Fukuyama, Francis, 3

full employment, democracy and, 113, 127, 136

Future of Democracy: A Defence of the Rules of the Game, The (Bobbio), 14–15

labor: capitalism compromise with, 115; democratic citizenship and, 109–10; dignity and, 9; equality and, 110–11; identity and migrant, 171–72; regulation of, 111, 128; safety and, 111; state generation of, 108; vulnerability in, 112; Workers' Statute, Article 18 and, 128–29. *See also* unemployment

Laffer, Arthur, 115

laicité, Italian public school and, 138–39

laissez-faire capitalism, 108

Larmore, Charles, 3

Later Works, The (Dewey), 39

Leaves of Grass (Whitman), 44–45

Lega Nord. *See* Northern League

liberal democracy, 15, 90

liberalism, 37–38, 158–59; cultural rights satisfied through, 166–67; defense of, 168–69; democracy compared to, 134; perfectionism and, 168; religious identity and, 165; taxation and, 124; universalism and, 81–82

liberal-pluralist paradigm, 15–16

libertarianism, 1, 76

liberty: as artificial construct, 133; Bobbio on peace and, 67; in contemporary societies, 46; cosmopolitanism and, 64–65; democracy and, 14–16, 103, 131; democratic cosmopolitanism and, 72; economic independence and, 117; equality and, 46; ideologies and, 51; individual and political, 54–55; political power and, 67–68; poverty and, 102;

Workers' Statute, Article 18 and, 128–29

Manin, Bernard, 59

Mansbridge, Jane, 58, 77

"many": democracy as compromise of "few" and, 102, 107, 130–31; "few," escalating tensions with, 100; financial crisis of 2008 impact on, 122; oligarchy and political power of, 100, 131; political parties, management of, 113; "trickle-down" economics for, 123–25

marriage, ethical life and, 177–78

Marshall, T. H., 115

Marx, Karl, 28, 114, 121–22; democracy and skepticism of, 135; nationalism, critique of, 36

Mattes, Margaret, 126

Mazzini, Giuseppe, 4, 69–71, 80

merit, 148–49, 151–56

meritocracy, 3, 151–52, 154

Meritocracy (Abravanel), 152

Miglio, Gianfranco, 171

migrants: citizenship challenges of, 81–82; human rights and, 7, 74–75; identity and labor of, 171–72; identity of EU with, 73; international conventions and aid for, 74; ownership and exclusion of, 87; public opinions on, 126; stateless, 73, 75–76; walls blocking, 27–28

militant democracy, 95

Mill, John Stuart, 4, 10, 37–38, 50, 117, 150–51, 153

moral-existential character, 82

moral universalism, 4, 63–64

Morgan, Edmund S., 42–43
multiculturalism: EU and, 82; political repercussions of, 165–66; public opinion on, 82–83; universalism and, 81–82
municipal socialism, 31–32
Murphy, John P., 39
mutation: of capitalism, 19; of democracy, 3, 34, 53; gated communities and, 29–30; identity and, 171–74; identity politics and, 23; ideologies and, 51; Italian public school and, 23–24, 26; signals of, 19–20; terminology of, 17–19. See also antiegalitarian mutation

nationalism: cosmopolitanism and, 80; in EU, 21, 87; globalization reaction of, 36; identity politics and, 28; Marx's critique of, 36; Northern League identity and, 22; racism and, 125, 173–74; universalism abandoned in name of, 80–81
national security, 66
Nazism, 51, 79
neofascism, 173
neoliberalism, 10, 99; antistate ideology and, 115; taxation critiqued by, 115–19
New Left, 159–60
normative-political character, 82
Northern League (Lega Nord), 6, 140; appropriation of rights and, 30–31; democracy and, 22–23; identity and, 170–71; nationalism, identity of, 22; regionalism and, 171

Nozick, Robert, 10, 116; on taxation as slavery, 123–24
Nussbaum, Martha, 3, 81, 116

Obama, Barack, 1, 11n2, 121, 145
occupation, 2
Occupy Wall Street, 14, 97, 122, 126, 132
Offe, Claus, 15
oligarchy: definition of, 97–98; in democracy, 98–99; "many" using political power against, 100, 131; poverty and law of, 130; "trickle-down" economics and, 125
Oligarchy (Winter), 97–98
1 percent, 14, 97, 100, 132
On Political Equality (Dahl), 56
ownership, exclusion of migrants and, 87

Pastore, Ugo, 175
patriotism, Bobbio and, 92
PCI. See Italian Communist Party
peace: Bobbio on liberty and, 67; democracy and possibility of, 106; Kant and importance of, 66
Peirce, Charles Sanders, 123
Phillips, Anne, 54, 58–60
Pierce, Charles Sanders, 38, 40
Piketty, Thomas, 8–9, 118, 122
Pinochet, Augusto, 100
Plato, 105–6, 151
pluralism: belonging valued over rights and, 176; democracy and, 14; EU and, 174; juridical, 52, 175–76; *laïcité* and, 138–39; religious, 145; in U.S., 174
Pogge, Thomas, 77
Polanyi, Karl, 17–19

polis, 105
political freedom, democracy and, 4, 10–11
political identity, 15, 75. *See also* identity politics
political parties, 58; decline of, 59, 119; in Italy, 60–61; "many" managed by, 113; "politics of ideas" and, 60; women disobeying, 62
political philosophy, 37–38, 46, 49
political power: democracy and, 5, 16; Kant on limits of, 71; liberty and, 67–68; of "many" against oligarchy, 100, 131; voting rights and, 24
political voice, social voice compared to, 54
Politics, The (Aristotle), 42
"politics of ideas," 59–61
Politics of Presence, The (Phillips), 58
"politics of presence," 59–62
populism, 1–2
possessive ideology, in EU, 14
postnation cosmopolitanism, 76, 78
poststate cosmopolitanism, 75–76, 78
poverty, 9; growth of, 111; liberty and, 102; oligarchy and, 130; rights and, 111–12; stigma of, 112
pragmatism, in U.S., 38–42, 48
Pragmatism: From Pierce to Davidson (Murphy), 39
private school. *See* Italian private school
privatization, 3, 10, 23, 136–37
procedural democracy, 160–61
Prodi, Romano, 142
Project for Perpetual Peace (Kant), 7, 64–65

proportional equality, 150
proportional representation, 58
protectionism, xenophobia and, 125
Przeworski, Adam, 100, 127
PSI. *See* Italian Socialist Party
public reason, 24–25
public school: democracy and centrality of, 24; public reason promoted by, 24–25; as right, 23–24, 26, 148; school vouchers for U.S., 144–45. *See also* Italian public school

Quest for Certainty, The (Dewey), 40
quotas, women and, 58–59

racism, nationalism and, 125, 173–74
Rawls, John, 3, 89, 115, 147, 149–50
Reagan, Ronald, 10, 115
reason, public, 24–25
reflective thought, 39
refugees, 7. *See also* migrants
regionalism, Northern League and, 171
Reimagining Political Community (Archibugi), 78
religion, 11; identity and, 164–65; Italy and equality of, 172–73
religious pluralism, 145
Renzi, Matteo, 129
representative democracy, 38; advocacy and, 57; equality and, 55; identification through, 56–57; justice in, 55–56, 58; "politics of presence" and crisis of, 62; voting rights and, 53–55; women and, 54, 56
reproductive power, women and, 163–64

Republic (Cicero), 63
Republic, The (Plato), 105–6, 151
republicanism, 70–71, 133–34
rights: ethnocentrists and,
    21–22; Northern League and
    appropriation of, 30–31; plural-
    ism and belonging valued over,
    176; poverty and, 111–12; public
    school as, 23–24, 26, 148; univer-
    salism of, 29; of working class,
    28–29
Risorgimento, 38, 80
Roma, 6, 83–84, 175–79
Roosevelt, Theodore, 1
Rorty, Richard, 39
Rosselli, Carlo, 4, 20, 38
Rousseau, Jean-Jacques, 4, 17, 64,
    67–68
rule of "wall," in U.S., 145

Saez, Emmanuel, 122
safety, labor and, 111
Santucci, Antonio, 39
Sarkozy, Nicholas, 83
Schmitt, Carl, 171
school vouchers, in U.S., 144–45
Schwartz, Joseph M., 146
secessionist movements, gated com-
    munities and, 6–7
security, national, 66
self-belief, 43–46
self-determination, 70
Sen, Amartya, 81, 116–17
September 11, 2001 attacks, 3, 66,
    122
Skinner, Quentin, 4, 50
Smith, Adam, 9, 64, 67, 152
social Darwinism, 108
social democracy: administration
    and, 32; in Bologna, 31–32; in

Italy, 114; paradigm of, 15–16;
    state and justice in, 114
social identity, 15
socialism, 31–32, 134, 158–59
social voice, political voice com-
    pared to, 54
Solon, 102–3, 107
South Tyrol, Italy, 166, 172
Soviet Union, 34–35, 134
Spartan model, gated communities
    and, 6–7, 30
Spencer, Herbert, 108
state: democratic cosmopolitanism
    critique and, 78–79; ethical, 88;
    free market advancing alongside,
    18–19; globalization and justice
    erosion in, 77–78; human rights
    violations in name of, 83–84;
    labor generated by, 108; social
    democracy and, 114; sovereignty
    of, 79
stateless migrants, 73, 75–76
Summers, Lawrence, 162

taxation: liberalism and, 124; neo-
    liberalism critique on, 115–19;
    Nozick on slavery and, 123–24
terrorism, 3
Thatcher, Margaret, 10, 115
Theory of Justice, A (Rawls), 149–50
Tocqueville, Alexis de, 4, 32, 49, 113,
    155; on democracy and individu-
    alism, 47; on equality in democ-
    racy, 48; U.S., journey to, 46–47
Togliatti, Palmiro, 93–94
Treaty of Rome of 1957, 7, 79–80
"trickle-down" economics, 123–25
Turchetti, Mario, 174
Tyranny of the Moderns (Urbinati),
    133

190   Index